T0330594

ROUTLEDGE LIBRARY EDITIONS: LABOUR ECONOMICS

Volume 12

WAGES AND EMPLOYMENT POLICY 1936–1985

WAGES AND EMPLOYMENT POLICY 1936–1985

RUSSELL JONES

Routledge
Taylor & Francis Group

LONDON AND NEW YORK

First published in 1987 by Allen & Unwin (Publishers) Ltd

This edition first published in 2019
by Routledge
2 Park Square, Milton Park, Abingdon, Oxon OX14 4RN

and by Routledge
52 Vanderbilt Avenue, New York, NY 10017

Routledge is an imprint of the Taylor & Francis Group, an informa business

© 1987 Russell Jones

British Library Cataloguing in Publication Data
A catalogue record for this book is available from the British Library

ISBN: 978-0-367-02458-1 (Set)
ISBN: 978-0-429-02526-6 (Set) (ebk)
ISBN: 978-0-367-02492-5 (Volume 12) (hbk)
ISBN: 978-0-429-39927-5 (Volume 12) (ebk)

Publisher's Note
The publisher has gone to great lengths to ensure the quality of this reprint but points out that some imperfections in the original copies may be apparent.

Disclaimer
The publisher has made every effort to trace copyright holders and would welcome correspondence from those they have been unable to trace.

WAGES
AND
EMPLOYMENT
POLICY
1936-1985

RUSSELL JONES
With a Foreword by Sir Alec Cairncross

London
ALLEN & UNWIN
Boston   Sydney   Wellington

**Allen & Unwin (Publishers) Ltd,
40 Museum Street, London WC1 1LU, UK**

Allen & Unwin (Publishers) Ltd,
Park Lane, Hemel Hempstead, Herts HP2 4TE, UK

Allen & Unwin, Inc.,
8 Winchester Place, Winchester, Mass 01890, USA

Allen & Unwin (Australia) Ltd,
8 Napier Street, North Sydney, NSW 2060, Australia

First published in 1987

British Library Cataloguing in Publication Data

Jones, Russell, *1959–*
   Wages and employment policy 1936–1985.
1. Labour policy – Great Britain –
History – 20th century
I. Title
331.12'5'0941   HD8391
ISBN 0–04–331110–5
ISBN 0–04–331111–3 Pbk

Library of Congress Cataloging in Publication Data

Jones, Russell, 1959–
   Wages and employment policy, 1936–1985.
Bibliography: p.
Includes index.
1. Wages – Great Britain – History – 20th century.
2. Great Britain – Full employment policies – History – 20th
century.
3. Unemployment – Great Britain – History – 20th century.
I. Title.
HD5015.J66   1987   339.5'0941   86–14143
ISBN 0–04–331110–5 (alk. paper)
ISBN 0–04–331111–3 (pbk. : alk. paper)

Set in 10 on 12 point Century Old Style by
Computape (Pickering) Ltd, North Yorkshire
and printed in Great Britain by Billing and Sons Ltd,
London and Worcester

Contents

Contents

Foreword

There was a time in the 1950s and 1960s when the problem of large-scale unemployment which had so troubled an earlier generation seemed at last to have been solved: and solved by governments in an effort of economic management that was quite new. In the 1980s the situation has changed. Unemployment in the United Kingdom is on a scale comparable with the peak rate in the early 1930s and shows no sign of rapid disappearance. Governments, once so eager to take credit for full employment, now protest that the level of employment is not their responsibility or that they are powerless to control it so long as workers go on pricing themselves out of jobs. A reaction against government intervention of any kind is in progress and is particularly strong against the very instruments of policy on which governments relied to manage the economy: swings in the budget surplus or deficit; restrictions on consumer credit; administrative controls of various kinds.

Underlying the change in mood and policy is public alarm at mounting rates of inflation. Inflation has continued ever since 1945 with periodic accelerations to a higher rate and has proved exceedingly difficult to subdue. It can no longer be attributed, as it might have been in the 1940s, to excess demand, for which obvious remedies exist. It now reflects an inflation of costs, both wages and raw materials, that may be little affected by the level of demand but has a momentum of its own. Wages in particular are now seen as presenting the toughest and most intractable obstacle to price stability because they are apt to go on rising at high levels of unemployment, as happened in the 1930s, and may increase sharply in years when an already high level of unemployment continues to rise. The more rapidly wages increase, the more rapidly prices rise too, so that wage earners may end up no better off. Indeed, many of them will be worse off if, as is likely, the government takes fright at the more acute danger that inflation will begin to get out of hand and adopts a more deflationary policy. The link between wage inflation and rising unemployment has then little to do with workers' success in securing higher *real* wages and pricing themselves out of jobs; it has a great deal to do with the zealous pursuit of higher *money* wages that ends up in faster inflation. It is the reactions of governments and financial markets to such inflation that contracts demand and creates redundancy and unemployment.

One of the merits of Russell Jones's book is that he traces what used to be called 'the Problem of Rising Prices' from the time when it was still hypothetical to its emergence as the dominant economic problem throughout the world. He shows how, from a very early stage, it was recognized by British economists that full employment would convey to the working population and their agents in the trade unions a potentially dangerous bargaining power that could not but extend to wage negotiations and could give birth to chronic inflation. The problem was much discussed during the Second World War; and when the war was over, ministers and officials sought an answer in committee after committee. In wartime it had been possible after the first big rise in wages to hold them at a fairly steady level with the help of food subsidies. Even after the war the trade union leadership practised considerable wage restraint and co-operated with the government in its initial effort in 1948 to introduce an incomes policy and in the freeze that followed in 1949–50.

If Gaitskell had had longer in office in the 1950s he would have tried to arrive at some more enduring arrangement, with what success it is impossible to say. As it was, the Conservative government took no initiative until the setting up of the Council on Prices Productivity and Incomes in 1957. This experiment in bringing outside opinion to bear on the collective bargaining process proved abortive but a few years later Selwyn Lloyd took the plunge, reviving the short-term policy of a freeze (or, as he called it, 'pause'), and coupling it with a new planning body in the form of the National Economic Development Council. This, too, was ineffective; but it started off a long succession of efforts to find a workable policy for moderating wage settlements, beginning with George Brown's Declaration of Intent.

The period after 1964 has been much more carefully studied than the events and ideas of earlier years. This part of Russell Jones's book is therefore less novel than the opening chapters but he has the advantage of reviewing later episodes in the light of earlier expectations and debates. One point that emerges strongly is that, throughout the long history of incomes policy, it was invariably discussed in the context of full employment, under governments publicly committed to preserve or restore full employment, never under a government threatening to repudiate, or having already repudiated, full employment. If any future government seeks to renew the search for an incomes policy, in whatever form, it is likely to do so as part of a programme of economic recovery. In such circumstances the question will be whether the TUC or any other body is in a position to restrain the upward movement of earnings as a contribution to such a programme or whether the only effective instrument for that purpose is the self-interest of employers as against the bargaining power of their employees. It cannot be taken for granted that the trade unions will be prepared to bargain lower wage claims (always assuming that they have sufficient unanimity and authority to enforce their side of the bargain) against a more expansionary fiscal and monetary policy. As far back as 1930 they disclaimed interest in wage concessions in the interest of higher employment.

A second feature of past experience has been the concentration of effort to arrive at an effective incomes policy at times when the chances of doing so were least. Again and again, efforts were made to restrain wage increases just when the momentum behind them was becoming irresistible. Similarly, the efforts ceased just when unemployment was about to rise fastest and furthest and workers' bargaining power was at its lowest. Yet earlier discussions might suggest that if the institutional arrangements necessary for an effective incomes policy are ever to be put in place with any hope of success it should be done before economic recovery has got well under way.

The story told in these pages is not a very hopeful one. It may well be that wages are almost as difficult to control as prices and that we must content ourselves with short, periodic freezes. However that may be, anyone contemplating a renewed attempt to reach a long-term solution will find much food for thought in the long record of past experience analysed by Russell Jones.

Alec Cairncross

*For Michaela
and her heaven-sent distraction*

Acknowledgements

There are a number of individuals without whom the publication of this book would have been impossible. First and foremost I would like to express my gratitude to my parents for giving up so much for my education. Secondly, I would like to thank Mr Frank Gregory and Mr Jack Cooke, my economics masters at the City of London School, who first fostered my interest in the subject and gave me such a sound basis on which to build. While at Bristol University I was lucky enough to be taken under the wing of Dr George Peden, whose knowledge, encouragement and help have proved invaluable over the last six years. Since my graduation I have been fortunate enough to work closely with Professor Sir Alec Cairncross and Lord Plowden, two of the most eminent postwar advisers to HM Treasury. I owe an enormous debt to their kindness and support. Numerous other people have been patient and gracious enough to talk to me about their experiences in public service, or to offer advice and comment. These include Lord Roberthall, Professor Sir Donald MacDougall, Professor Stanley Dennison, Lord Croham, Lord Trend, Lord Roll, Professor Sir Austin Robinson, Miss Nita Watts, Mr Neil Rollings, Dr Rodney Lowe and Dr Jim Tomlinson. Finally, I would like to thank the archivists at the Public Record Office in Kew, Congress House, Nuffield College, Oxford, and the British Library of Political and Economic Science for their help, and offer my congratulations to Mrs Sylvia Allan, Miss Michaela Economides and Mrs Eve Jones for their skill in deciphering my handwriting.

Russell Jones
March 1986

1

Introduction

The writing of this book is the result of two preoccupations of mine: a fascination with John Maynard Keynes and his economics, and what I see as the urgent need to provide an adequate historical explanation for the present situation whereby Keynesian principles have been cast aside and policy is in the hands of a government pledged to monetarist techniques of economic management. Fifty years ago, with the publication of *The General Theory of Employment, Interest and Money*, Keynes seemed to offer not just Britain, but the world as a whole, a feasible explanation of the massive unemployment of that time and a means (short-run demand management) by which it could be, if not removed, then reduced considerably. Keynes's explanation, as he expressly intended, rapidly became accepted by many economists and by 1939 few academics could claim not to have at least seriously questioned the assumptions they held about the way the economy operated. Moreover, by the end of the Second World War, the British coalition government, heavily influenced by an influx of specialist economists into Whitehall during the hostilities, had released the now famous White Paper on *Employment Policy*. This document pledged future administrations to 'accept as one of their primary aims and responsibilities the maintenance of a high and stable level of employment, and although it still contained a number of important reservations and qualifications, endorsed the use of many of the basic tools and principles embodied in Keynes's *magnum opus* to achieve that end.[1] Thereafter, economic policy came to be run very much on Keynesian lines by both major political parties. The commitment to 'high and stable employment' soon became a commitment to 'full' employment, and this was retained until 1975 when the Labour government of the time felt obliged temporarily to suspend the commitment in view of the extenuating economic circumstances then prevailing. It has not reappeared since then although the use of financial policy to offset, at

1

Table 1.1   *Postwar Unemployment in the UK*

	Average mid-year seasonally adjusted total excluding school-leavers	*Percentage of working population*
1945–50	341,600	1.6
1951–5	301,300	1.25
1956–60	370,800	1.5
1961–5	412,800	1.6
1966–70	528,600	2.7
1971–5	736,900	2.8
1976–80	1,325,900	6.2
1981–5	3,008,100	11.0

Source: Central Statistical Office, *Economic Trends* (London: HMSO).

least partially, short-run fluctuations in aggregate demand was retained until 1979 when the Callaghan Labour administration was replaced by Mrs Thatcher's Conservative administration. For at least the first two decades of the postwar era, unemployment, although showing a gentle upward trend, remained negligible. As Table 1.1 illustrates, it only really began to climb steeply after 1975.

Since 1979, Keynes and Keynesian policies have been abandoned and the maintenance of full employment has been formally dropped from the government's list of specific policy objectives. In 1981 the Treasury told the House of Commons Treasury and Civil Service Committee that 'it has become abundantly clear . . . that governments themselves cannot ensure high employment'.[2] We have seen in recent years the neo-liberal economic theories of American economist Milton Friedman and his British disciples to the fore. Economic policy is today aimed at the maintenance of a stable long-term and non-inflationary macroeconomic environment through strict monetary control and fiscal rectitude, and at the need to make markets as free and competitive as possible. Government intervention in the economy has become a dirty word and we have in many ways returned to a conventional wisdom thought to have been put aside for ever after the Second World War. If unemployment began to climb steeply after 1975, since 1979 the escalation has been yet more dramatic and alarming and at the time of writing (November 1985) we are faced with a problem of mass idleness unequalled since the very worst years of the interwar depression. At present more than 13 per cent of the total potential workforce is

2

without a job and in some of our cities, particularly those in the old industrial areas, the rate is over 25 per cent. For most of the postwar era few if any economists or politicians would ever have expected unemployment again to reach such dizzy heights, but this is indeed the case now and many would agree that the figures are likely on present policies to get worse before they get better. The fact that with this unemployment has come poverty, a wave of civil unrest and violence and a deepening of divisions in society does not augur well for the future.

All this begs the questions, 'What went wrong with the Keynesian era?', 'Why did it come to an end?' and 'Why are we now faced once again with the enormous waste and misery of mass unemployment?'

The major reason for the abandonment of Keynesian economic policies in Britain was their association with unacceptable levels of wage inflation and successive balance of payments crises. Throughout the first two decades of the postwar era Britain witnessed creeping inflation and a tendency for wages to outstrip productivity growth, but between the mid 1960s and mid 1970s the problem became increasingly worse and eventually reached proportions not normally associated with a developed country. In the twenty years from 1947 to 1967 prices doubled. They doubled again in the period 1968 to 1975. Indeed in 1975, in the aftermath of the first OPEC price shock, and the last wholehearted and, by the standards of the 1950s, unsuccessful attempt to secure full employment, the rate of inflation reached close to 30 per cent. By the general election of May 1979 the problem, while reduced, was but slightly less disturbing to the public, and the electors returned to power with a large majority a Conservative government determined to run the economy in a non-Keynesian way and to rid the country of inflation. It was as Dr Alan Budd of the influential London Business School has put it, the 'searing experience' of inflation which lay behind the Thatcherite Revolution in policy-making, just as the 'searing experience' of interwar unemployment led to the Keynesian Revolution in economic policy-making in the first place.[3]

It is the changing nature of government attitudes and policies towards the problem of wage inflation which this book seeks to investigate. In the following chapters of historical narrative I hope to be able to show the following:

- How much were the inflationary failings of a Keynesian full employment policy foreseen by those at the epicentre of the initial conver-

3

Table 1.2   *UK Average Price Inflation (per cent per annum)*

1945–48	2.8	1967–9	4.2
1949–51	5.0	1970–72	7.6
1952–4	4.7	1973–5	16.4
1955–7	4.4	1976–8	13.6
1958–60	1.6	1979–81	14.4
1961–3	3.2	1982–4	6.1
1964–6	4.0		

Source: Central Statistical Office, *Annual Abstracts of Statistics* (London: HMSO)

sion to Keynesian principles within the government machine, and what measures did they put forward to deal with the problem? Thomas (Lord) Balogh, for example, has alleged that the problem of wage inflation in a full employment economy was 'dismissed' until the early 1960s,[4] while Abba Lerner has stressed that it took us four decades to progress from 'a state of innocence of the inflationary dangers of full employment to a state of obsession with them'.[5] Do these statements accurately and truly sum up the position in the early years of the Keynesian era?

– How did policy and thinking with regard to dealing with the wages problem develop over subsequent years as the Keynesian scheme became more firmly established as the basis for economic policy-making in this country?

– Why did the measures taken to ameliorate the wages problem keep failing? What were the mistakes made in policy formulation and what were the underlying reasons for those mistakes?

– Is there a future for Keynesian economic policies, or are we faced with monetarism for ever more? More specifically, what help can this historical narrative offer us in regard to the solution of the wages problem in the context of a new era of Keynesian policy-making? This question is particularly relevant given the widespread concern and disillusionment with the results of the monetarist era.

In many ways the book forms a history of British incomes policy or action designed to restrict collectively bargained wage increases to levels required to bring about a reduction or elimination of wage inflation. The arguments for and against various forms of incomes policy still command an enormous amount of space in books, academic journals and indeed daily newspapers. Formal incomes policy is seen by

4

present-day Keynesians as a necessary component of any remotely realistic alternative to Thatcherite economic policies, and indeed by some more sympathetic to the government's cause as a useful complement to the present policy regime in that it would help to offer a better division of money national income between jobs and prices. As long as the key question in economics remains 'How can we drastically reduce unemployment without causing a surge in inflation?', the matter of how to make an incomes policy work will remain relevant. It is only by an adequate understanding of past failures that we shall be able to offer any hope for the future. This book will I hope contribute to providing this understanding.

The layout of the book is as follows: it is divided into nine more chapters beginning with a brief description of *The General Theory* and Keynes's treatment of wage inflation in it, together with some comment on the initial reception of *The General Theory* in the Treasury. The next chapter looks at the development of thinking on employment and wages in Whitehall during the war in relation to both the mobilization of the economy for the duration of the hostilities, and also the planning undertaken for peace, which began in 1941. Thereafter successive chapters are allocated to the wages problem in employment policy as it developed during each period of office served by a particular political party, beginning with Attlee's postwar governments and ending with the present Thatcher administration. The final chapter seeks to formalize my conclusions in the light of the questions listed above. Chapters 2–5 draw extensively on material available in the Public Record Office in Kew, together with other primary source materials, including the Trades Union Congress (TUC) records and various unpublished diaries and private papers. Chapters 6–9, because of the thirty-year rule on the release of government documents, use sources which are predominantly secondary in nature and I have frequently had to draw extensively from certain individual works. Any originality in this work tends therefore to be confined to the earlier chapters. However, I have also made use throughout the book of a number of interviews which I have conducted with various government officials and advisers of the last forty years or so.

2

The General Theory, the Treasury and the Wages Problem 1936–9

The General Theory

Ignoring the restocking boom which followed the First World War, unemployment in the United Kingdom averaged some 10 per cent of the workforce throughout the interwar period and reached close to 16 per cent in 1932. Government figures, which at that time dealt only with the insured population, suggested an even higher average, with a peak of some 22 per cent at the worst point of the slump. Even allowing for the inadequacies of earlier sources of unemployment figures, this marked a not inconsiderable escalation of unemployment over the pre-1914 average.[1]

The experience of high and prolonged unemployment, and all the poverty and deprivation that went with it, cast a long shadow over what Keynes christened 'Classical economics'.[2] Nevertheless, this school of thought, encompassing the notion of a self-regulating economic system tending to full employment ('Say's Law'), 'sound finance' and the severe limitations of public works expenditure, still retained a firm hold over the economic policy-makers in the early 1930s.[3] Keynes, who had been conscious of anomalies in the Classical system since the mid 1920s, set out in *The General Theory* to present a comprehensive and coherent critique of this analytical framework and to replace it with a viable alternative which would yield policies to ameliorate the national and international slumps and usher in a new period of long-term prosperity.[4] In doing this he proferred a disequilibrium model of capitalism which implied that full employment was, in fact, a special case.

According to Keynes, the Classical theory of the labour market depended on two postulates, which together entailed that the economy was at full employment. These were, first, that 'the [real] wage is equal to the marginal product of labour' and, secondly, that 'the utility of the [real] wage when a given volume of labour is employed is equal to the marginal disutility of that amount of employment'.[5] To the Classics the problem during the Great Depression was that, by introducing rigidities into the labour market, the trade unions had prevented their members' wage rates achieving the equilibrium level and so had created 'voluntary' unemployment. A reduction in money-wages, which would lower costs and prices, and increase total demand, was mooted as the only thoroughgoing solution to the unemployment problem.

Keynes criticized this analysis by asserting that even if an all-round reduction in money-wages could be effected (which both he and many more orthodox economists thought highly doubtful), this solution presupposed constant aggregate demand, which he believed to be an absurdity. His conclusion was that apart from in the export sector, money-wage reductions could only have a positive influence on employment indirectly through the fall in the rate of interest produced by the reduction of cash balances required for transactions purposes, and via expectational effects.

In his alternative system, which encompassed 'involuntary' unemployment, Keynes, while rejecting the second Classical postulate, endorsed the first and thus agreed with the Classics that a decline in the real-wage rate was a *sine qua non* for the increase of employment. If the economy was not at full employment, which he thought most likely, this should be remedied by increasing aggregate demand and prices by a combination of reducing, and keeping low, long-term interest rates, and fiscal expansion. The degree of emphasis to be placed on the latter should increase with the depth of the slump. Keynes's belief in the efficacy of fiscal policy, and loan-financed public works in particular,[6] supported by his theories of the 'multiplier' and 'liquidity preference' was, of course, also a significant break with the past and Classical theory.[7]

Keynes's employment policy depended for its success upon the prediction that 'whilst workers will usually resist a reduction of money-wages, it is not their practice to withdraw their labour when

7

there is a rise in the price of wage goods', except when such an inflation-induced decline in real-wages 'proceeds to an extreme degree'.[8] This seemingly illogical view was explained by the supposition that 'the effect of combination on the part of a group of workers is to protect their relative wages'. Thus, while money-wage reductions, because they 'are seldom or never of an all-round character',[9] were thought to lead to stern worker resistance, reductions in real-wages generated by moderate inflation, which 'affect ... all workers alike', were not.

Most latter-day economists, following Leontieff,[10] have subsequently supposed that Keynes's acquiescence postulate was derived from an assumption that workers were subject to 'money-illusion' or 'the failure to perceive that the dollar, or any other unit of money, expands or shrinks in value',[11] while Keynes seems to have viewed the asymmetry in workers' behaviour as constituting a rational course of conduct born out of the fact that an expansion in demand does not affect a worker's relative real-wage. It is noticeable that Leontieff was hard-pressed to establish proof for his interpretation of Keynes's message from textual evidence.

Keynes's analysis of inflation in *The General Theory* was very much bound up with the concept of 'excess-demand', or a level of total demand in the economy above and beyond that necessary to secure full employment. But it is inaccurate to state, as many textbooks have done in order to simplify *The General Theory*, that he presumed the existence of a perfectly elastic aggregate supply curve as long as unemployment existed, and a perfectly inelastic aggregate supply curve as soon as full employment was reached, so that only at full employment would prices rise, and by the full amount of any excessive increment of demand. Besides this position of 'true inflation', Keynes also identified positions of 'semi-inflation', encountered prior to full employment. These were determined, he thought, by the heterogeneity of equipment, the fact that inelastic supply of all goods and services is not reached simultaneously, the degree of increase in aggregate demand (since this influenced the time period within which modifications and extensions to equipment could be made) and, most importantly of all from our point of view, the 'natural' upward movement in money-wages motivated by the 'psychology of workers'. Keynes believed that increased aggregate employment generated an intensification of the struggle for a higher relative wage, and increased trade union bargaining power. In connection with the greater willingness of employers to grant wage increases during periods of rising profits and output, this represented an inflationaly force 'of considerable practical significance' that could absorb part of any increase in aggregate demand, but Keynes did not think it would be sufficiently active to undermine his acquiescence postulate.[12]

So, in *The General Theory* Keynes was dismissive of the trade unions' ability to render a full employment policy nugatory by demands for increased wages. He neither adhered to the modern monetarist tenet that workers always bargain in real terms and will sooner or later realize they have suffered a decline in real-wages and act to counter this, nor did he believe, as do many modern Keynesians, that sustained high levels of employment exert such an intensification of the struggle for a high relative wage among the trade unions as to push wages to a level inconsistent with the maintenance of this position in the absence of a further, accommodatory, expansion of demand. Keynes described the 'leapfrogging' theory of wage inflation, but he believed it would operate within limits.

Lord Kahn, a member of the 'circus' of economists involved in discussions of the *Treatise of Money* which led to the early drafts of *The General Theory*, and a great friend and inspiration to Keynes, has described Keynes's treatment of wage inflation and its interconnection with the level of employment in *The General Theory* as 'unsystematic and unsatisfactory'.[13] Given the varied interpretations of Keynes's analysis and other complaints as to *The General Theory*'s ambiguities in this respect,[14] coupled with the fact that Keynes's relative-wage hypothesis approach to wage determination was inconsistent with his 'absolute income' theory of the consumption function,[15] there is much to be said in support of Kahn's critique.

Kahn attributes the shortcomings of Keynes's analysis of the labour market to his preoccupation with convincing people of the injustice and inefficacy of money-wage reductions as a means to combat the unemployment problem, and the belief that unemployment would never fall to a low enough level for wage inflation to prove a serious problem.[16] Both of these explanations have their merits. While Keynes did envisage the realization of high employment through demand management at this time, that is to say some 95 per cent of the workforce, given care and planning in the construction of policy,[17] apparently he did not foresee as practicable the levels of employment approaching 98 or 99 per cent of the working population which existed in this country for much of the postwar period. He did indeed devote much effort to trying to show how reductions in money-wages merely served to deflate demand and, in a closed system, could only raise employment through the rate of interest and expectational effects. What is more, it is now obvious from his correspondence and later writings in the 1930s that Keynes became aware of his brevity in the treatment of the wages problem at higher levels of employment, and the 'perhaps rash generalisations' he had made in *The General Theory* in this respect.[18] Not much more than a year after the publication of *The General Theory* Keynes was planning to publish a second book entitled *Footnotes to 'The General Theory of Employment, Interest and Money'*. He further admitted that Chapter 2 of *The General Theory*, which contained his 'acquiescence postulate', was 'the portion of my book which most needs to be revised'.[19]

However, there was, I believe, another equally fundamental explanation of the particular approach to the wages problem adopted by Keynes in *The General Theory*. Keynes was referring to the real world as he perceived it and wanted it to be, but unfortunately, in comparison to his knowledge of finance, his understanding of the collective bargaining process was in 1936 rather limited. Misguidedly, Keynes implicitly incorporated his own 'Liberal-Victorian' philosophical belief in full employment as the *sine qua non* of a civilized and contented society[20] into his model of worker psychology. Unfortunately for Keynes, what he and other 'Keynesians' have described as 'selfishness' or 'irresponsibility' in the conduct of wage bargaining has proved a much more potent force than has 'reason', simply because workers have in reality increasingly sought to maximize non-'Keynesian' utility functions, incorporating a greater emphasis on the maintenance and improvement of individual real-wage levels, and less on relative real-wages and high levels of employment.

II
Reactions in Whitehall

The balance of evidence suggests that despite the policy advice of outside economists in the Economic Advisory Council Committee on Economic Information being of a broadly Keynesian nature from 1932, the 1930s saw only an easily overestimated, gradual and very incomplete transition to the tenets of Keynesianism within the Treasury, which, from the abandonment of the gold standard in 1931, had taken over from the Bank of England as the focal point for the co-ordination of economic and financial policy.[21] Thus, while senior officials had accepted a limited counter-cyclical role for public works expenditure in 1937, and by 1939 had become more conscious that the budget could be used to manage demand, they still remained unconvinced by the 'multiplier' theory and, fearful that a budget deficit would result in the withdrawal of funds from productive employment, they favoured raising interest rates to dampen down economic activity in a boom and, perhaps most importantly of all, made no attempt to utilize the kind of national income accounting framework, eventually taken up in 1941, that Keynes believed so vital for the effective management of the economy.[22]

In addition to these stumbling blocks of a theoretical nature, weighty political considerations and massive administrative obstacles also barred the way to a wholesale conversion to Keynesian economic analysis in the later 1930s. Even though the political pressures against public works diminished after 1936, as they gained increasing support among economists and politicians of diversified political colours,[23] the Treasury was still heavily influenced in its thinking by such factors.

For example, the Treasury and more orthodox economists were convinced that Keynes underestimated the role that domestic and international confidence could play in undermining his policies.[24] While Keynes was not completely insensitive to the fact that high spending would be viewed as profligacy and a threat to financial stability in many circles, his lack of political responsibilities and his personal temperament and philosophy made him pay less attention to these opinions than the Treasury officials, who were paid to consider the widest implications of policies, and were, above all, haunted by the spectre of the 1931 financial débâcle. Thus, though the Treasury was willing to countenance considerable 'window dressing' of budgets to make them more acceptable to institutional opinion,[25] it refused to endorse any deliberate unbalancing, apart from in the extenuating circumstances thrown up by rearmament and war. The balanced budget rule of thumb acted as an implicit assurance to city, financial and industrial interests that the natural profligacy of politicians in a democratic setting would be constrained. As Sir Frederick Phillips, a senior Treasury official, put it, a budget deficit 'is difficult to reverse and completely out of control'.[26]

On an administrative level, throughout the 1930s, the volume of capital investment directly undertaken by central government as a percentage of total domestic fixed capital formation and as a percentage of gross domestic product (GDP) was much smaller than that undertaken by local government, so that large-scale counter-cyclical regulation of public investment would probably have become the responsibility of local authorities.[27] A decision to adopt such a programme would have necessitated either a system of grants to local authorities, or a major restructuring of the financial relations between the core of government and the localities. Any fiscal stabilization policy requires speed of action to be effective and thus for it to have been realized would have necessitated the setting-up of a central body with widespread powers to co-ordinate and control investment plans. As the Treasury was still far from convinced of the efficacy of the Keynesian medicine, there was an understandable reluctance to establish any such body, with its massive repercussions on the make-up of British politics and government. On the other hand the central government U-turn over spending plans in the period 1929–31 had made local government authorities wary of exhortations for increased expenditure, so that it was possible that even increased grants would not have proved an adequate fillip to capital development.

Following the publication of *The General Theory* academic economists as diverse as Joan Robinson, John Hicks, James Meade, David Champernowne, Friedrich von Hayek, A. C. Pigou, and Hubert Henderson all criticized Keynes's 'acquiescence postulate' or sought to extend his treatment of the wages problem at high levels of employment.[28] However, given the climate of opinion within Whitehall, one would not expect to find many, if any, explicit references from 'insiders' to the inflationary repercussions of a Keynesian policy regime designed to sustain a high level of employment. This is indeed the case. Even though Sir Ralph Hawtrey, the Director of Financial Enquiries, and the only civil servant in the Treasury who could in any real sense be described as an 'economist' at this time, actually wrote a critique of *The General Theory* for general circulation within the Treasury in 1936, he concentrated on Keynes's definition of savings and investment and the role of monetary policy, and made no comment about his assumptions regarding trade union psychology and wage inflation.[29]

As a theoretician, Hawtrey was still very much more entangled in 'Classical' or more specifically 'Marshallian' economics and, indeed, he had found great difficulty in coming to terms with much of Keynes's new schema. At the same time, he had no reason to believe, despite rearmament, that levels of employment much above those prevalent in 1937 were likely to be forthcoming in the immediate future.

12

There was, however, a considerable escalation in government expenditure and borrowing in pursuit of rearmament in the late 1930s and contingency plans were drawn up for the transition to a war footing. From late 1936 apprehension grew over the threat of inflation, particularly as officials believed that 'the economic and financial strength and soundness of this country is little less vital to us in an emergency than ships or aeroplanes or guns',[30] and even though close to 10 per cent of the workforce remained idle throughout this period.[31] The inflationary problem owed much, as the government itself was aware, to the prolonged recession of the previous fifteen years or so, which had produced a shortage of skilled labour, especially in the building and engineering industries.[32] The result was that, despite the agreement between the government and trade unions over the dilution of skills, signed in March 1938, the competition for resources produced by general recovery, a building boom and the particularities of rearmament demand led to 'bottlenecks' and pressures which manifested themselves in price increases.

While most internal government discussion focused on the pure demand-pull aspect of this inflation and efforts were made to co-ordinate the demand for armaments with supply capacity as much as possible, both ministers and officials were also conscious to some extent of the threat of a price-wage reactionary spiral and industrial unrest. For example, in 1937, Neville Chamberlain, then Chancellor of the Exchequer, remarked how

prices are bounding up now . . . All the elements of danger are here, increasing cost of living, jealousy of others' profits, a genuine feeling that things are not fairly shared out and I can see how we might easily run in no time into a series of crippling strikes, ruining our programme, a sharpening of costs due to wage increases, leading to the loss of our export trade, a feverish boom followed by a disastrous slump.[33]

In a similar vein, Sir Richard Hopkins, a second secretary at the Treasury, warned that

the danger is . . . from the efforts of the salaried and wage-earning classes to secure compensation for higher expenditure in terms of higher incomes. The rising cost of living is almost as potent a factor as unemployment itself in producing social unrest.[34]

Furthermore, Sir Frederick Leith-Ross, the Chief Economic Adviser to the government, asserted that 'we must at all costs avoid getting involved in the vicious spiral of increased costs and increased depreciation of currency'[35] and in so doing pointed out risks that were chronically underestimated by policy-makers and advisers as recently as the early 1970s.

Inflation was also identified as a major problem in the mobilization of the British economy for the First World War and as a result contingency plans to meet this threat in any future hostilities were drafted as early as 1929 and updated over the following years. Initially the major emphasis in memoranda was on the need for wage-fixing as a complement to fiscal and monetary action to restrain prices. As time progressed, the Ministry of Labour, haunted by the industrial unrest of the last war and mindful of the need to obtain the optimal distribution of labour, succeeded in shifting the accent in preparations to a continuation of voluntary collective bargaining in connection with firm policies of taxation and price and profit control.[36] Obviously officials were convinced that a wage-price spiral was a certainty in the face of a consistently high and accommodating level of demand, unless drastic steps were taken.

Thus, even though the 'Keynesian Revolution', for political, administrative and purely theoretical reasons, was anything but complete in government circles in the late 1930s, we can conclude that there was in officials' and ministers' statements on financial policy, and in the contingency plans for war, at the very least, an implicit scepticism about Keynes's attitude to the wages problem in a full employment economy as expressed in *The General Theory*. It should be underlined, however, that there was no explicit statement to this effect from policy-makers.

3

The Control of Wartime Inflation and the 1944 White Paper on Employment Policy

Wartime Inflation Control

During the war the British economy was mobilized to an extent unmatched by any other belligerent, provoking exceptional pressure on resources and the reduction of unemployment to negligible proportions. Of all the aspects of wartime economic policy, the discussions relating to the formulation and implementation of a policy to keep prices in check are especially relevant to this study. The relative success of the measures used to combat inflation over the period of hostilities came, understandably, to colour attitudes within government and trade unions when it came to planning for a peacetime wages policy. Thus it would be useful to take a more detailed look at this particular aspect of the war economy.

Historical experience, not least that of the First World War, during which prices more than doubled, pointed to the danger of considerable inflation manifesting itself over the course of the war. Obviously, because of the repercussions for living standards, labour relations, the escalation of foreign debts and general disruption of the efficacy of the economy and public confidence, this was something the government wished to avoid. As early as November 1939 Lord Stamp's Survey of Financial and Economic Plans (which advised the Chancellor) noted how many wage increases had already been granted and how many more were being demanded; in consequence it urged the Ministerial Economic Policy Committee to abandon the plans for wages laid down before the war and promote a system of centralized review and authorization of wage rates. Objections to such a strategy were again voiced by the Ministry of Labour, on similar grounds to before, and also as a 'Central Wage Tribunal' might well produce the very result it was hoped to avoid, the regular review of wages on a cost of living basis. Eventually it was decided by ministers to put before the National Joint Advisory Council (the tripartite body dealing with labour problems that had been set up in October 1939) and authoritative account of Britain's financial position with a view to breaking the link between wages and the cost of living index.

Initial efforts to 'educate' the trade unions in the realities of war finance, the threat of a vicious spiral and the need for sacrifice achieved little apart from a promise to go away and consider the problem. Ernest Bevin, then still the General Secretary of the Transport and General Workers' Union (TGWU), was of the opinion that he had the right to defend the interests of the men he represented and press for wage increases to compensate for price increases, and Sir Walter Citrine, the General Secretary of the TUC was convinced that the rank and file would reject the government's proposals for sacrifice, and instead suggested the encouragement of voluntary national savings, an idea not viewed by the Treasury as being in itself a viable solution to the problem.[1]

Despite much internal discussion of the wages question, and the onset of the second phase of a wage–price spiral, the government's policy remained, apart from *ad hoc* price subsidy, largely one of 'wait and see', until the National Joint Advisory Council (NJAC) formally replied to the proposals of the previous December. In the mean time the Churchill coalition came to power, and with it Bevin, who at the Prime Minister's request was found a parliamentary seat and took over as Minister of Labour and National Service.[2] Finally, in June 1940, the NJAC rejected a new proposal from Bevin, who had been converted just prior to taking office to the need for a fall in working-class living standards, for wage stabilization subject to a four-month review and voiced its support for a continuation of voluntary collective bargaining. However, the council did favour one important change, in the form of the reference of unsettled disputes to a National Arbitration Tribunal, whose settlements would be binding. At the same time strikes and lock-outs would become illegal unless the difference of opinion had not been acted upon by the Minister of Labour within twenty-one days of his being informed.[3]

From this point of the war onwards, and in particular after the 'Stabilisation Budget' and White Paper on *Price Stabilisation and Industrial Policy* of 1941,[4] the government's wages and inflation policy was built increasingly upon the interdependent foundations of trade union moderation and responsibility, strict control of the old 1913 cost of living index via price subsidies, profit regulation, an extension of rationing on the basis of 'fair shares for all', and a more rigidly planned fiscal policy. This is not to deny, however, that Bevin at a ministerial level, Lionel Robbins in the Economic Section of the Cabinet Office, and Ministry of Labour officials, still had to fight off several attacks on free collective bargaining over the following eighteen months from those who desired either centrally fixed wages, or a definite commitment from the unions to the stability of wages in return for the stability of prices.[5] Indeed, in the difficult circumstances of December 1940, even Keynes suggested that a wages policy of the latter nature would be a useful additional weapon in the fight against inflation.

Keynes's greatest contribution to the reorientation of wartime anti-inflation policy came in the form of the budgetary practice he forwarded. Being acutely aware of the inherent danger of a vicious spiral of wages and prices, Keynes at the beginning of the war was expanding his ideas on inflation as set out in *The General Theory*. In articles published in *The Times* in November 1939, and subsequently as a pamphlet, 'How to Pay for the War', Keynes launched a vigorous attack on the government's budgetary policy.[6] He condemned the traditional assessment of revenue according to the principle of what the taxpayer could bear as inadequate in the context of wartime conditions, and turned conventional analysis on its head by first estimating the national income and its component parts and from this determining the capacity for war-making and the necessary level of taxation needed to transfer that part of the national income to the government without creating inflation. At the then existing levels of national income and taxation, he calculated an 'inflationary gap' of from £1,000 million to £1,100 million. To eradicate this, he suggested tax increases of a predominantly regressive character, made more acceptable by promises to repay part of them after the war as 'deferred pay', and in the form of family allowances. A redistribution of income from workers to manufacturers was, according to Keynes, inevitable. It could be realized by inflation, or by planning and consultation.[7]

17

Throughout the winter of 1939–40 Keynes publicized his plans and subjected them to open debate. Initially he was criticized from inside the government on the basis of his taxation proposals. Left-wing opinion, recalling the broken promises of the First World War, favoured finance of the war by heavy taxation of the rich and a capital levy.[8] Moreover, Sir Robert Kindersley of the National Savings Movement was also critical, asserting that the savings movement 'trusts the people, and he [Keynes] does not'.[9]

Though none of Keynes's proposals were included in Sir John Simon's 1940 budget, support for Keynes grew when the Churchill coalition came to office, as labour's resistance to his ideas weakened in the face of Britain's increasingly desperate military position, and as Keynes and economists sympathetic to him were drafted into civil service departments. In the September of 1940 the Central Economic Information Service started work on estimates of the national income and by the winter references can be found in Treasury memoranda to the size of the 'inflationary gap'.

The 1941 budget marked a key turning point in wartime economic policy and, indeed, in modern economic history. This was the first Keynesian budget presented in national income terms and it was accompanied by a White Paper setting out estimates of the national income, expenditure and the 'inflationary gap'.[10] While the figures were probably unreliable,[11] the principle was sound and the remaining war budgets were presented in a similar format, though in reality borrowing rather than inflation was utilized to a greater extent, and with greater effect, than Keynes anticipated.

Government anti-inflation policy was by no means completely successful in eradicating excess demand-induced price increases, and had not a much stronger and more powerful trade union movement exerted considerable restraint, there would have been little hope of containing inflation.[12] As it was, the self-imposed incomes policy meant that only average earnings showed any substantial increase during the war. Nominal wage rates rose more slowly than the real cost of living, albeit faster than the official index, which working people were well aware was grossly unrepresentative.[13] In addition there was nothing like the number of days lost through strikes and disputes seen in the First World War.[14]

It seems reasonable to believe that the social and welfare provisions secured by workers and their families, not least at the behest of Ernest Bevin, had a not inconsiderable effect in engendering responsibility in wage bargaining, in addition to the price stabilization policy and the other measures mentioned above. There was, for example, provision of school meals, of nurseries for working mothers and of cheap milk for children and expectant mothers, together with other dietary supervision, the establishment of factory canteens, doctors and welfare workers, a significant change in the attitude to those who required state assistance of any kind, and a reluctance to direct labour. As Titmuss said,

it would, in any relative sense, be true to say that by the end of the war the government had, through the agency of newly established or existing services, assumed a measure of direct concern for the health and the well-being of the population which, by contrast with the role of the government in the nineteen-thirties, was little short of remarkable. [15]

What conclusions relevant to the thinking on the postwar wages problem in employment policy can we draw? There is no doubt that the war re-emphasized the dangers of a high level of demand as far as inflation was concerned, especially in conjunction with a trade union movement intent on maintaining its level of real wages. Nevertheless, policy-makers and academics in general were shown how wage restraint and a not inconsiderable degree of industrial peace had been achieved within the general context of a continuation and extension of prewar bargaining machinery, price and profit control and social reform.

Overall, the experience of wartime wages policy seems to have lessened the degree of trepidation and increased the degree of optimism surrounding future attempts to deal with the wages problem in a high employment economy. But one must ask how relevant a projection of wartime trends in union behaviour was to the prospect of a peacetime, high employment economy. Price and profit control in connection with rapid social reform was all very well in wartime, but would it be politically possible in normal peacetime conditions? What was the quantitative effect on wage bargaining of the atmosphere of common sacrifice produced by total war? How great an impact would the growth of trade union power and influence have on wage claims? All these questions would still have to be asked when formulating wages policy for the postwar years.

II
The Employment Policy White Paper of 1944

The examination of postwar economic policy began in earnest in 1941. While Keynes was in Washington negotiating 'Lend–Lease', the Treasury had preliminary discussions on postwar internal problems, but these had not advanced far when more pressing matters intervened. It was left for the economists in the Economic Section of the Cabinet Office to keep up the momentum in this direction for some time. According to Lord Robbins, it was John Jewkes who first suggested that a paper should be prepared on postwar employment, and James Meade, who needed little or no encouragement, started work on this as early as February 1941.[16] This paper was circulated in July 1941 under the title 'Internal measures for the prevention of unemployment'.[17] Together with the preliminary Treasury deliberations, it played a major part in the organization of the Inter-Departmental Committee on Post-War Internal Economic Problems and was one of the first papers discussed by this body.

Meade's paper dealt with banking, investment consumption and budgetary policies appropriate to maintaining a level of demand for labour sufficient to offset any decline in the demand for labour of particular occupations, and it was on these matters, and on the need for an appropriate external policy, that debate centred over the next three years. However, Meade also made it clear that demand management would necessitate an absence of excessive wage increases. 'A wage policy,' wrote Meade, 'which refrains from insisting upon rapidly rising wage rates, except in so far as increases in productivity permit, is . . . a necessary condition for a successful effort to prevent . . . unemployment.' Failure to realize this policy would, he thought, mean that 'the attempt to reduce general unemployment would have to be abandoned'.[18]

Throughout 1942 there were numerous references in Economic Section discussion papers on the postwar period to the threat of a vicious spiral of wages and prices in association with a high level of employment, especially in those documents drafted by Meade.[19] However, it was a Ministry of Labour memorandum which produced the most in the way of ideas to counter this threat, even though at this time this memorandum was considered neither by its authors, nor by the Inter-Departmental Committee on Post-War Internal Economic Problems, to be 'in the first class of priority' and was not discussed until late in 1942.[20]

20

The first draft of this memorandum was completed in January 1942, but at this stage it contained no reference at all to a Keynesian employment policy. A copy was sent to Robbins with a covering note from Sir Frank Tribe, a senior official in the Ministry of Labour, which admitted that 'some of the economics may be rather amateurish' and asked if Robbins could point out 'any definite . . . fallacies'. The memorandum was basically a history of the wage bargaining process from the First World War onwards, followed by some tentative suggestions and recommendations for the postwar period. As might be expected, given the ministry's opinion on wage control in the late 1930s and the early war years, it came down firmly in favour of free collective bargaining.[21]

Thereafter, further informal talks took place between Tribe and Robbins and with Treasury officials, too. The final draft, circulated during June 1942, contained a new section, 'The effect of wages policy on policy for the prevention of slumps', based substantially on a note from Robbins to Tribe which reiterated Meade's prognosis of the previous year. It was made clear that 'a moderate wage policy is a *sine qua non* of a successful anti-depression policy'.[22]

The final draft also included reference to the threat of inflation in the transition. It recognized that a continuation of compulsory arbitration, providing it could be agreed upon by both sides of industry, would be very welcome in respect of this menace, and in noting the 'vital importance' of stabilization policy in controlling wages, the document added that 'our general object after the war should be to avoid, so far as possible, violent fluctuations in the cost of living'. However, it concluded that if there should still be a tendency for wages to escalate, some system of state control might have to be imposed. Finally, there was mention of how automatic indexation of the cost of living could be a prime mover in setting up a vicious spiral and nullifying exchange rate adjustment; conclusions reached by Keynes and Robbins the previous year.[23]

The circulation of this memorandum and Robbins's informal dialogue with Tribe seem to have resulted in Robbins asking for utterances on the wages problem from Marcus Fleming and Stanley Dennison in the spring of 1942, while Meade had already reiterated his views on the matter to the section.[24] All three economists believed that if unemployment were reduced to around 5 per cent of the workforce, wages were likely to rise 'uncomfortably fast'. Keynes also viewed 5 per cent as the 'minimum practicable level of unemployment' at this time.[25] All the

21

economists in the Economic Section questioned on the matter agreed that voluntary collective bargaining was the optimum means of fixing wages from the point of view of industrial peace, but forwarded moderating influences of varying degrees to temper the inflationary bias of the process. Dennison thought that an education programme, outlining to trade unions the general economic situation and the implications of excessive wage demands, would be enough to secure restraint. In contrast, Fleming thought government-guided emphasis on 'reasonable' settlements 'should be avoided like the plague' and suggested instead a voluntary, or if necessary, statutory, upper limit on wage increases, somewhere in the region of 5 per cent per annum, made more acceptable by the limitation of dividend increases to the same degree, and stronger legislation on monopolistic pricing. Meade also warned that 'the imposition of maximum wage rates may be desirable to prevent monopolistic wage earners ... preventing the proper development of employment ... and to prevent a high general demand for labour from leading to the danger of an inflationary vicious-spiral'.[26] He added that a job evaluation plan might be the best means to overcome the difficulties of controlling wages in detail, if this was deemed necessary.[27]

The Treasury's approach to postwar employment policy formed a stark contrast to that of Meade and the Economic Section. In October 1941 senior officials in the Treasury actually went so far as to canvass Economic Section opinion about a policy of deflation after the war. In its presentation to the Inter-Departmental Committee on Post-War Internal Economic Problems, drafted by Sir Hubert Henderson, and oddly entitled 'The post-war relation between purchasing power and consumer goods', the Treasury was lacking in firm recommendations for economic management over the transition period, beyond a resolution to be flexible and a commitment not to appreciate the exchange rate by internal deflation, as had been done after the First World War.[28]

It was not until 1943 that ministers came to analyse seriously postwar employment policy. The publication of the Beveridge Report saw the Cabinet's Sub-Committee on Reconstruction Priorities interested to ascertain whether Beveridge's assumption of 8.5 per cent unemployment was a practical possibility, especially as the official figures then utilized implied that the average annual level of unemployment in the 1930s had varied between 22.1 per cent in 1932 and 10.8 per cent in 1937. This concern led the Economic Section to draft a memorandum entitled 'The maintenance of employment' for the sub-committee.[29] This paper, though still based on Meade's preliminary work, was more of a joint effort than the 1941 paper.[30]

Prior to the drafting of this memorandum, Meade had in fact tried to bring about the preparation of a 'Keynes Plan' on postwar employment, in a similar vein to the Beveridge Report. The idea was still-born, as Keynes himself thought that the subject was 'very much more mixed up with external policy' than the Beveridge Report had been and required less formal planning, and as aspects of the policy were already being dealt with.[31]

There was an emphasis throughout the development of 'The maintenance of employment' on a continuation of a 'moderate' wages policy linked to productivity improvements in connection with efforts to sustain demand. However, as a result of the doubts expressed by Fleming and Meade as to the likely success of such a policy, reference was also included in the final draft to the possibility of having to impose 'some limitation upon the rate at which wage rates might be raised', or abandoning the policy of high employment altogether.[32]

When the Economic Section memorandum reached ministers, the Chancellor, Sir Kingsley Wood, complained it 'went too far in the direction of treating unemployment as a single problem for which one solution could be found'.[33] As a result, all the interested departments were asked to undertake further studies on employment policy and a committee of senior officials was set up, with the Permanent Secretary to the Treasury, Sir Richard Hopkins, as chairman, to collate the results of the various inquiries into a single comprehensive report for ministers. This body began its deliberations in the autumn of 1943.

There was but limited reference to wages policy in the departmental memoranda for this committee. This deficiency derived from two factors: a consistency with the Economic Section's belief in a combination of a 'moderate' wages policy, and the fact that this aspect of employment policy was, as yet, by no means a burning issue. It was widely held that a slump similar to that of 1920–1 and of the early 1930s would occupy postwar governments' attentions rather than a long-term boom, with all its implications for effective demand and inflation. Lionel Robbins summed up official opinion in this regard in 1943:

One thing, however, is tolerably certain, sooner or later there will come some slackening of the pressure of necessary demand in so far as that is spontaneously generated, and in so far as counteracting measures are not taken, the phenomena of boom will give way to the phenomena of depression.[34]

Moreover, there was still to be settled the fundamental division of opinion between the broadly Keynesian Economic Section and the more traditional and cautious approach to employment policy of most Treasury officials.

The Economic Section memorandum of earlier that year had described the employment problem as 'essentially' one of maintaining expenditure and assumed 'an effective mobility of labour' to prevent the so-called 'structural unemployment' of the interwar era. The section desired measures to affect consumption, and in particular Meade's idea of the variance of social security contributions, as an additional and automatic counter-cyclical device, in view of the inappropriate nature of public investment for such a task. The Economic Section also thought 'it worth while incurring some deficit in the budget to offset a depression' and suggested that there was something to be said for balancing the budget over a period in excess of the 'traditional year'. By contrast, the Treasury, echoing the Economic Advisory Council Committee on Economic Information's investigation of the slump in 1935, regarded structural unemployment as being as important as, if not more important than, 'demand-deficient' or 'cyclical' unemployment. Treasury officials were also sceptical of Meade's social security scheme and still both very conscious of the administrative difficulties of a counter-cyclical investment programme and convinced that the 'indefinite continuance of unbalanced budgets ... would give rise to distrust, and ultimately threaten stability and employment'.

The frustration of the Economic Section with the Treasury's attitude is well summed up by the following extract from a paper prepared for the steering committee:

In various papers put forward to the Steering Committee the Treasury has rejected almost all the proposals put forward by the Economic Section . . . with a view to stabilising aggregate demand at a high level . . . If that view were to prevail the role of the State in respect of cyclical unemployment would be essentially passive. The State would refrain from aggravating the depression by mistimed campaigns for economy, but would take no positive steps to relieve it. This conclusion seems to us unduly pessimistic.[35]

The 'Report of the Steering Committee on Post-War Employment',[36] completed in January 1944 and drafted by Hopkins, was a remarkable compromise between the two schools of thought and a perfect example of the senior civil servants' expertise in drafting. While it endorsed demand management and the national income approach to economic policy, it did not sanction budget deficits, or any specific employment target, which, it was feared, might generate over-ambitious expectations and become a 'political football' in the context of the wartime coalition.[37] The report also noted the problems that the international environment could present for internal policies, the various difficulties in controlling each constituent part of aggregate demand and the complexities of the transition. In short it favoured an internal anti-slump policy involving a long-term public investment programme, with variations in taxes on investment and consumption as a further measure if necessary, all within the context of a balanced budget. The steering committee report represented a victory for the Economic Section, though by no means a comprehensive one, and in part this was merely because Hopkins's interpretation of the steering committee's terms of reference directed attention primarily to the problems of a low general level of investment and consumption demand.

It was not until the sixteenth meeting of the steering committee that Robbins was called upon to prepare a memorandum on wages and prices.[38] A slightly revised version of Robbins's initial memorandum forms almost verbatim the section on wages policy in the steering committee's report, and it is not difficult to notice the consistency of this document with previous Economic Section work on the subject.[39]

Chapter III of the report began with the statement that

It is an arithmetical truism that the volume of additional employment that will be generated by a given volume of additional expenditure will be greater if wage rates are constant than if they are rising.[40]

It went on to note the difficult choice that could be faced, and indeed was faced so often in subsequent years, by governments when money-wages showed an upward tendency.

When, however, employment has reached a reasonably high level, an absence of relative stability in rates of remuneration is more probable, if rates in general increase at more than a certain rate . . . either one must be prepared to allow, and if necessary promote, an inflationary increase in money expenditure and prices in order to maintain employment, or else one must set limits to the increase in expenditure, at the cost of a decline in employment. We are at the point at which there is a real danger of a vicious spiral.[41]

The report judged that the tendency for high wage claims would emerge from the loss of the check that fear of unemployment imposed on wage demands and from the increased disposition to run risks wrought by higher unemployment benefit. The problem was purported to be of little or no consequence provided that wages rose in tandem with, or slightly in excess of, the rate of growth of productivity, as gradually rising prices were viewed as a means to reduce the burden of debt and were historically associated with periods of prosperity. Both comprehensive central wage-fixing and the imposition of a maximum wage norm in conjunction with central arbitration were mentioned as means to arrest any excessive upward movement in money-wages, but ruled out in the short term because of the great administrative and political difficulties involved and because it was felt that free collective bargaining deserved a trial period.[42]

The steering committee report dealt with the wages problem fairly briefly and not in overly technical terms. While it noted the danger of a changed attitude in trade union bargaining practices and the possibility of 'real-wage resistance', it remained cautiously optimistic in its outlook. It is this optimism which demands closer attention, as I shall outline in relation to the White Paper which developed from the steering committee report.

Early in 1944 the Coalition government was in a hurry to pre-empt Beveridge's private report on *Full Employment in a Free Society* by releasing its own statement on the subject.[43] Hopkins, however, though he thought the steering committee had taken a 'middle course' between the two poles of opinion among 'insiders' on the merits of Keynesian economics, was not convinced of the adequacy of the report for a White Paper, not least because of developments in international economic policy and the limitations they implied for exchange rate adjustment in particular. There followed considerable debate over the drafting of the White Paper and it eventually contained increased emphasis on the special problems of the transition, structural unemployment and the balance of industry. It was not until mid May 1944 that the War Cabinet came finally to endorse the White Paper. Despite the fact that at the time the White Paper was being drafted, the biggest strikes of the war were going on (in the engineering industry), the section on wages and prices was also based predominantly on the line taken in Robbins's memorandum of the previous December.[44] It took the form of an exhortation to the effect that 'workers must examine their trade practices and customs to ensure that they do not constitute a serious impediment to an expansionist economy and so defeat the object of a full employment policy'. But most important of all, however, was the emphasis in the document that the commitment to 'high and stable' employment was limited, being conditional on 'reasonably stable' wages and prices. The explicit nature of this qualification seems to have resulted from pressure from Sir Hubert Henderson, then an economic adviser to the Treasury, who in spring 1944 was very worried that the employment policy might prove incompatible with a balanced external account and that devaluation would only provoke a wage-price spiral. In March Henderson warned that if, as he believed the Economic Section wished, 'we commit ourselves to pursue policies designed at all costs to avert a downward movement [in prices], the result might be to perpetuate an upward one'. He believed that the absence of strict conditions pertaining to the behaviour of wages and prices was 'reckless and pointless'.[45]

As far as specific measures for the stabilization of prices were concerned, there was general agreement among 'insiders' that the wartime policy should initially be extended into the transition period, in connection with rationing and other controls. However, the majority thought that long-term price control of a comprehensive nature was undesirable or unworkable, though Robbins, for one, did see an important role for it as an anti-monopoly instrument, and there is evidence that other economists favoured the subsidy of the prices of certain essential goods. The White Paper stated that the government was prepared to do what it could to stabilize prices in the long run, without making specific commitments, and urged employers to seek 'in larger output rather than higher prices the reward of enterprise and good management'.[46]

There was widespread agreement among the economists and civil servants in Whitehall that the wages problem was essentially political in nature, and the limited commitment to maintenance of 'high and stable', but not excessive, employment in the White Paper can be viewed as a form of 'social contract'. Officials hoped that wage restraint and discipline in price and profit policies would be forthcoming in exchange for high employment and output *per se*. But while 'insiders' seem to have been almost unanimous in their acceptance of this as the best possible solution to the wages problem and were willing to see it tried out, some officials and economists retained doubts as to whether or not the sanction of a non-accommodatory effective demand policy, operating on an aggregate level, could prove a successful deterrent to each component part of the labour market. The question was asked whether in the long run, even supposing that every negotiating group accepted that if all pay rose by more than 2 per cent there would be unemployment, would that stop a particular group from going out straightaway

27

and asking for more? It would be fine if all groups were to say, 'If we did that it would be bad for us all: so we won't do what we don't want others to do.' But some groups might say, 'Let's get our rise quickly before other groups follow suit.' A sanction that is operated by an aggregate is not necessarily a certain deterrent to any one component, especially as if aggregate pay does rise faster than money GDP, it was not necessarily true that the groups or individuals who would suffer unemployment would be the ones that pitched their claims too high. However, there was also no consensus as to what represented a viable alternative to the limited commitment. [47]

Robbins was one of the most optimistic about the limited commitment, as the following extract from his autobiography indicates:

I could never believe [statutory wage and price control] to be sensible. I do, of course, believe that it is essential for the government to have a prices and incomes policy as regards its own employees . . . but it never seemed to me to be likely that, save as shock tactics in a grave emergency, an attempt to control wages all along the line . . . could do more good than harm . . . I believe that in the end they [the unions] will learn habits of greater responsibility and do less harm to the general working of markets if they are left free to make their own policy . . . and their own mistakes. [48]

Meade, as might be expected given his earlier statements on this area of policy, while in favour of a limited commitment, was less optimistic about its success, and just prior to the publication of the White Paper, in a note to Robbins, he reiterated his concern that because of 'uncontrolled inflation . . . we might have to give up the employment policy'. [49] In contrast to this, Fleming still believed that the only solution to the wages problem lay in the 'imposition of centrally defined maximum wage norms or . . . some form of collectivist solution'. [50]

The final composition of the policy for wages outlined in the White Paper seems to have had its roots in five major and interrelated factors. Primarily, there was the general optimism derived from the war experience of trade union wage restraint, which, despite the engineering strikes of 1944, remained a potent force. Secondly, while 'insiders' were by no means unaware of the effect rigid price and profit control had exerted on wage claims, they seemed willing to believe that restraint could be extended into the postwar period, even though they could not expect to maintain, nor did the majority of officials wish to maintain, anything like the degree of control exerted over prices and profits in wartime in the long run. No doubt the lack of an explicit and assertive TUC statement on this matter prior to the drafting of the steering committee report and the issue of the White Paper made it easier to acquiesce in this belief. Thirdly, there was the suggestion that many of the economists and officials, of whom the most obvious example was Robbins, had inherited not only Keynes's economic theories but also his philosophical outlook towards employment, with the result that they too came to equate the degree of working-class contentment and well-being with the level of employment. Next there was the widely held opinion that another slump, similar to that of 1920–21 and 1929–33, in that considerable downward pressure would be exerted on prices and wages, was likely to occur in the not too distant future. It was thought that the major problem after the transition was likely to be stopping prices and wages falling, rather than their inflation. Finally, there was the fact that no other single policy could be agreed upon and, in any case, each suggested alternative represented such an enormous political risk and administrative burden as to be deemed a non-starter. For example, any form of direct control over the labour market gave rise on the one hand to fears of widespread industrial unrest and political strikes, and on the other hand represented to many people a not insignificant step towards autocracy.

In June 1944 the Reconstruction Advisory Council (the tripartite body set up to allow both sides of industry to survey reconstruction plans with the coalition) met to discuss the general issue raised by the White Paper on *Employment Policy*.[51] Sir Walter Citrine recorded that he was sure that the TUC would welcome the government's shouldering of responsibility for 'high and stable' employment. The TUC General Secretary was making it clear that the consensus of opinion within his organization was that above all it was the government who should be responsible for the maintenance of employment.[52] But at this forum the trade union representatives held back to a large degree from raising more detailed comments and criticism and it was only with the publication of the TUC's *Interim Report on Post-War Reconstruction*, towards the end of 1944, that their full attitude to the White Paper, and the fragile foundations of the government's 'moderate' wages policy, became apparent.[53] This document declared that the TUC not only wanted a commitment to full, rather than 'high and stable', employment, but that its members also had no intention of shouldering the bulk of the burden of sacrifice necessitated by such a target for its own sake, as the following extracts exemplify.

The TUC would not at any stage commit itself in advance to approve or acquiesce in the methods to be adopted to reach full employment simply because those methods can be shown to be well-fitted and even necessary to the achievement of that objective . . . In short, the TUC would have at all times to consider whether it was, on balance, better that the objective should be modified rather than that methods incompatible with the rights of work people and the objectives of Trade Unionism should be used to achieve it . . . There is no need to fear . . . a [wage–price] spiral if the government can convince the movement that in genuine pursuit of a policy of full employment it is determined to take all other steps that are necessary to control prices and convince the trade union movement of the need to secure equivalent guarantees that wage movements will not be such as to upset the system of price control.[54]

While it is certain that aspects of this report were looked at by some ministers and by officials in the Ministry of Labour as plans went ahead to bring the new employment policy to fruition, it seems that little attention could be paid to them in the context of the wartime coalition. Hugh Dalton made this clear to the TUC Economic Committee in spring 1945, stating that 'there were no early prospects of any effective action being taken on the [TUC's] proposals in the absence of a Labour Government'.[55] This conclusion, together with the desire to give the employment policy as it stood a chance, meant that the trade unions' pronouncements had no immediate effect on government strategy.

III
Keynes and the Plans for Postwar Employment Policy

In this depiction of the development of plans for postwar employment and wages policy, the name of Keynes has been conspicuous by its absence. In 1943 and 1944 Keynes was busy preparing plans for a multilateral solution to the problems of the international economy in the interwar years, which eventually bore fruit in the form of the Bretton Woods-International Monetary Fund (IMF) system of international payments. As a result, he had little time for formal discussion and analysis of postwar internal employment policy. What he did contribute was mainly confined to backing Meade's scheme to vary social security contributions in a counter-cyclical manner, compiling estimates of the postwar national income in collaboration with Richard Stone and participating in Treasury discussions on the form of the postwar budget.[56] However, Meade has claimed in a book published in 1982 that Keynes was 'very conscious' of the danger of an upward drift in

30

wages in conjunction with sustained high unemployment.[57] But Meade makes no claims about Keynes being in favour of formal wage restraint in the postwar period. Meade's conclusion in this respect has been verified by his colleagues to whom I talked and is also corroborated by Keynes's wartime writings in academic journals and correspondence.

As mentioned above (p. 17), Keynes did suggest using a wage stop in late 1940 as an additional means of ensuring that the vast increase in government expenditure dictated by the needs of war did not translate itself into inflation, but it would be wrong to transfer this judgement directly from the context of the war economy, with its extreme pressure on resources, to a peacetime high employment situation. This policy was seen by Keynes merely as an emergency expedient in the pressure-cooker environment of 1940–41, and in view of his doubts over the practicability of increasing taxation and voluntary saving to close the 'inflationary gap'. For example, in another memo-randum at this time Keynes wrote, 'The freedom of the wage bargain is the Ark of the Covenant for the Trade Union Movement, which it is not wise to call in question except for some grave and unavoidable cause.'[58]

From his somewhat limited writings on the postwar wages problem one can identify two main strands to Keynes's thoughts. First, there is the confident assertion that the mere realization that the problem exists will bring about an eventual solution. Thus, in an article in the *Economic Journal* on international price stability, he wrote:

Some people argue that a capitalist country is doomed to failure because it will be found impossible in conditions of full employment to prevent a progressive increase in wages. According to this view severe slumps and recurrent periods of unemployment have been hitherto the only effective means of holding efficiency wages within a reasonably stable range . . . The more conscious we are of this problem, the likelier we shall be to surmount it.[59]

Secondly, in line with his Whitehall colleagues, there was the emphasis Keynes attached to the internal political nature of the problem, which rendered it unsuited to rigid theoretical solutions. In a letter written late in 1943 Keynes emphasized that his 'central point' was that 'the task of keeping efficiency wages reasonably stable . . . is a political rather than an economic problem'.[60] In another *Economic Journal* article published late in the following year Keynes wrote:

Of course I do not want to see money-wages soaring upwards . . . It is one of the chief tasks ahead of our statesmanship to find a way to prevent this. But we must solve it in our own domestic way, feeling that we are free men, free to be

31

wise or foolish. The suggestion of external pressure will make the difficult problem of making good sense prevail still more difficult.[61]

Finally, we are referred by both Lord Kahn and Sir Austin Robinson to a letter written by Keynes as editor of the *Economic Journal* to the author of an over-formalistic article on the problem of inflation, in which Keynes stated:

I do not doubt that a serious problem will arise as to how wages are to be restrained when we have a combination of collective bargaining and full employment. But I am not sure how much light the kind of analytic method you apply can throw on this essentially political problem.[62]

So, Keynes admitted on several occasions during the war, in line with a re-examination of his acquiescence postulate in the late 1930s, that sustained levels of high employment would generate an annoying and worrying rate of wage inflation, but I think it would be wrong to assume that he believed it would ever become out of hand. He was confident that future governments would not pursue a policy of feckless deficit budgeting or note issue, and he could not believe that the working class could be so 'irresponsible' and 'masochistic' as to sterilize policies designed to maintain employment. Thus he wrote the following in 1945 on the future of the employment policy.

It may turn out I suppose that vested interests and personal selfishness may stand in the way. But the main task is producing first the intellectual conviction and then intellectually to devise the means. Insufficiency of cleverness, not of goodness, is the main trouble.[63]

As far as a solution to the wages problem was concerned, Keynes had little concrete advice to offer beyond a warning against an overly rigid approach and an emphasis on the need for some sort of political device, perhaps along the lines of his own scheme for dealing with inflation during the war. In the mean time it seems that Keynes was quite happy to go along with the recommendations and policies outlined in the steering committee report and the *Employment Policy* White Paper. Certainly he offered no explicit criticism of the sections on wages and prices in either document and pronounced himself in agreement with the overall content of both.[64]

It should be made clear that Keynes never put forward on paper any ideas that could be definitely interpreted as the framework for a formal, peacetime incomes policy such as we have experienced on occasions since the war on the advice of Keynesian economists.[65] However, given the great man's fertility of mind, and his abhorrence of both inflation and unemployment, [66] it is possible that had he been alive for another decade or so, he might have changed his tack in this respect as levels of employment above and beyond the 95 per cent of the workforce that he suggested might be practicable were realized, sustained and looked upon as a necessity for the retention of political power. This is by no means certain, however, as towards the end of his life, in the face of various economists of a more radical ilk claiming to be 'Keynesian', Keynes came to re-emphasize his belief in certain fundamental elements of Classical economics. This is particularly true of his pronouncements on external policy. If this reawakening of the Classical spirit extended to his attitude to internal policy, as Professor Dennison believes, it is more likely that Keynes, like his contemporaries Robertson, Hawtrey and Henderson, would have fought a battle in the postwar period against those who favoured running economy at too high a level of employment, especially for political gain. [67]

4

Wages Policy and the Attlee Governments

The Labour Party came to power in the summer of 1945 with a firm commitment to 'full' as opposed to 'high and stable' employment. This it hoped to realize by a combination of the techniques outlined in the 1944 White Paper and the rather nebulous concept of 'democratic planning'. Its pre-election propaganda, however, failed to touch on the wages problem in any detail. The Labour Party's report on *Full Employment and Financial Policy* stated that inflation should be checked by an extension of wartime controls.[1] Its election manifesto neglected even to mention the word inflation. It merely promised to maintain the value of money and to retain certain controls for the sake of 'fair shares'.[2]

Attlee's first administration was faced immediately with a series of dilemmas in regard to employment and wages policy. In the first place there was a fear that some structural unemployment might develop as demobilization progressed.[3] Labour's commitment to full employment implied that this should not be allowed to become excessive. Secondly, the economy was bloated with excess demand and suppressed inflation inherited from the war. It was imperative that inflationary pressure was restrained to protect the fragile external account devastated by Britain's war effort, while the government also had to be wary of puncturing recovery. Thirdly, there was a need to channel labour into occupations consistent with peacetime demands. The problem was that the relative wage levels required to do this might be partially or wholly offset in an inflationary manner by wage claims aimed at consolidating wartime gains in relativities, or at compensating for the decline in earnings after the war.

A first interdepartmental 'Working Party on Wages Policy' was authorized by Sir Edward Bridges, the Permanent Secretary to the

Treasury and Secretary to the Cabinet in October 1945,[4] and over the next six years wages policy was rarely out of the limelight at any level of government. It ran through five phases which may be summarized as follows.

I
Phase I: 1945–8

The first phase covered the period to February 1948. During this time the government issued regular exhortations for moderate wage-bargaining, while emphasizing the need to allow peacetime industry to develop. Generating the optimum relative wage structure was as important as keeping the absolute wage level down. Besides cabinet ministers making innumerable speeches on the subject, the government reconstituted the wartime tripartite NJAC in the late spring of 1946 as an educative forum where the new and wider responsibilities of the trade unions and employers under conditions of full employment could be made clear.[5] A *Statement on the Economic Considerations Affecting Relations between Employers and Workers* (Cmd 7018) was also released in January 1947, but this document proved to be rather a timid affair. Paragraph by paragraph discussions with the NJAC resulted in considerable censorship. It contained rather less emphasis on wages than on keeping costs competitive. Subsequently the Minister of Labour, George Isaacs, reported to a colleague that it had not been easy to get agreement on the paper – the TUC was particularly difficult.[6]

Two groups of opinion within Whitehall made clear their dissatisfaction with wages policy at this time. At a ministerial level, Emanuel Shinwell (Fuel and Power), with the support of Aneurin Bevan (Health), took the initiative in trying to obtain a better integration of manpower planning, as espoused in various published and unpublished 'Economic Surveys', and wages policy, through minimum wage legislation and the creation of a national authority, or central wages tribunal, to make specific recommendations on wage levels in individual industries.[7] At the same time, James Meade and others in the Economic Section of the Cabinet Office were convinced that 'the peculiar difficulties of wages policy . . . were due in large measure to . . . general inflationary pressure, and that it was essential . . . to do everything that was feasible to move towards a condition of greater balance between supply and demand, including reducing food subsidies'.[8]

In 1947 Chancellor Hugh Dalton's November budget considerably reduced the excess of demand over supply, but little formal action was taken to strengthen wages policy until 1948. The moderate views of the Ministry of Labour held sway, not least because Isaacs was an ex-union official and could argue with the backing of personal experience, and because Ernest Bevin was his most vocal supporter in Cabinet.[9]

II
Phase II: 1948-9

The second phase of wages policy began in earnest in February 1948 with the issue of the *Statement on Personal Incomes, Costs and Prices*.[10] In the midst of the 'Convertibility Crisis' the Prime Minister had made a strong appeal to workers in all industries and employments not to press for increases of wages, or changes in conditions which would have a similar effect.[11] At the same time a Working Party on the Stabilisation of Wages was set up to consider what further steps could be taken prior to discussions with both sides of industry.[12]

Though the working party reported in September 1947, discussions as to what represented the optimum statement to make on wages policy continued for four more months.[13] Numerous radical proposals for checking wage inflation were put forward for consideration including making the NJAC bear responsibility for, or at least express a published view on, major wage claims, the imposition of a public sector wage freeze, the imposition of a universal and statutory wage freeze, the allocation of a government representative to all major wage negotiations, and the setting up of a 'Central Appeal Tribunal' to which claims considered to be against the national interest could be referred.[14] All of these were, however, rejected. The final version of the White Paper, issued without the prior consent of the TUC, followed the Ministry of Labour line and accepted the undesirability of direct interference by the government in wage negotiations.[15] Instead it called for a voluntary freeze of wage rates (and of 'incomes from profit, rent or other like sources'), except where an undermanned industry could not attract labour in any other way, and where productivity had increased. The document also underlined that collective agreements should be strictly adhered to and that wage increases would not necessarily be taken into account in the control of prices and margins.[16]

The TUC was somewhat resentful about the lack of consultation immediately prior to the White Paper's release, but nevertheless called a special executive conference in March to discuss the policy. The conference backed the policy with two provisos. It was insisted that workers 'below a reasonable standard of living' and those who sought to maintain established differentials be able to apply for wage increases also. The latter was a reason for wage increases specifically rejected in the White Paper.[17] Subsequently the government persuaded the Federation of British Industries (FBI) to accept voluntary dividend limitation and further extended its policies of price subsidy and control. Furthermore, in his first budget speech Sir Stafford Cripps announced a 'once and for all' capital levy on investment income for those earning in excess of £2,000 per annum.

Allowing for the fact that the four exceptions to the general rule could potentially have exempted every trade union, by the spring of 1948 the Labour movement had committed itself for the first time to a policy that was in many ways contrary to its *raison d'être*. The policy was monitored closely at both a ministerial and official level and was widely regarded as a qualified success. Indeed, early in 1949 there were discussions about issuing a follow-up document to publicize the moderating influence the *Statement* had exerted on wage bargaining. This idea was not, however, taken up; instead the Chancellor merely drew attention to the reduction in wage inflation in his budget speech. A month later Attlee reaffirmed the policy of wage restraint in an answer to a parliamentary question.[18]

III
Phase III: 1949–50

The third phase of wages policy began towards the end of 1949. August 1949 saw the establishment of another official working party. It was asked to consider how wages and prices policy could be used in conjunction with public expenditure and investment cuts to preserve the relative cost advantage to be derived from devaluation and to make room for increased export production. Its frame of reference was short-term. Officials eventually decided on a further voluntary freeze of wages for at least six months, but this time it was hoped to cast the net of the policy rather wider, and in particular to include the 1.5 million workers whose wages were linked directly to the cost of living through 'sliding scales'. More stringent price control and an extension of voluntary dividend limitations were also recommended. The working party specifically rejected Cripps's suggestion that all wages, prices and profits be frozen by statute for three to six months, both because of the administrative burden it implied and on the grounds of the political and legal burdens involved. An idea floated by the Ministry of Labour that taxation of employers should be used as a sanction against wage claims was thrown out for similar reasons.[19]

Initial ministerial consideration of the report and discussion with the TUC resulted in the inclusion of an increase in profits tax in the package and the exemption of especially low paid workers. After several further meetings with Cripps, Bevin, Bevan and Isaacs a new and tighter wage policy received the endorsement of senior trade unionists. On 23 November 1949 the TUC General Council announced its recommendation of a one-year stabilization of wage rates, and that cost of living agreements should be suspended, provided the retail price index did not increase by more than 5 per cent. Despite Bevin's observation that the narrowing of skilled and semi-skilled workers' differentials effected by the 1948 pay guidelines had already caused great unrest, and his antipathy to the further exemption of low-paid workers from the freeze, this single exception to the general rule was retained.[20]

The TUC called another special executive conference in January. With a general election imminent, delegates voted narrowly in favour of the policy.[21] Its moral authority was, however, tenuous and few expected the policy to last. By the spring Cripps was debating whether or not to try to consolidate the freeze through budgetary concessions. Vincent Tewson, the General Secretary of the TUC, advised Cripps against this course as he did not believe the unions would recognize the notion of the social wage. In his budget speech Cripps was content to pay 'a very high tribute' to the trade unions for their wage restraint over previous years and to ask for continued forbearance.[22] At the end of June, just as the Korean War began, the TUC General Council announced that, while it still backed general restraint, it must in view of the discontent of skilled and semi-skilled workers, the improved performance of the economy, the length of time that voluntary restraint had been maintained, and the need to protect living standards

adopt the practical course of recognizing that there must be greater flexibility of wage movements in the future.[23]

Bevin's fears had thus proved well founded.

38

IV
Phase IV, 1950–51

Though Cripps was disappointed by this announcement, the 1949 freeze had always been viewed as a temporary measure. Indeed a further thorough review of wages policy had been progressing in Whitehall for six months. The fourth phase of wages policy was already under way. There was a growing belief in Whitehall that inflation, rather than unemployment, would become the major postwar problem.[24] Previous wage policies were seen as being too *ad hoc* and short-term, and a long-term or semi-permanent means to make collective bargaining conducive to full employment without inflation was sought. As an Economic Section memorandum put it,

the assumption has always been that the trade unions were being asked to exercise special restraint because of special and temporary economic circumstances.[25]

Discussions were to continue for a further six months on what was known to officials as 'Operation Prospero' before a policy thought suitable was put to the unions. Cripps and his successor Hugh Gaitskell, together with the Economic Section and the Central Economic Planning Staff were at the centre of the debate. Investigations were made into the wages policies in operation in Scandinavia. There was also a lot of support at all levels for the encouragement of incentive schemes. These, it was thought, would help to link wages to productivity, reduce conflict over differentials and relativities and develop a minimum wage, especially if they were coupled with a single, independently developed and reviewable job evaluation scheme. Such claims were not, however, supported by any worthwile initiatives on how the trade unions could be persuaded to accept such schemes, nor was there any analysis of their implications for the spread of workplace bargaining and the successful policing of wage restraint.[26] Arguments for state wage-fixing resurfaced too, only to be dismissed as involving too many loopholes and complexities, and as no such system would be accepted as compatible with the British way of life.[27] The NJAC was roundly criticized for failing to fill effectively its prescribed role. Bevan dismissed it as an unwieldy and conservative body,[28] while Cripps concluded that it had not yet developed in such a way as to make available for collective bargaining purposes sufficiently full economic information in a form most suitable for use in the determination of wages and conditions.[29] As in debates in previous years, it was suggested that a wholly new advisory body be assembled to issue guiding lights and briefings with a view to educating workers with regard to their wider responsibilities under conditions of full employment. In the end this approach was thought to best meet the criterion, as Sir Edward Bridges put it, 'that any wages policy initiative should preserve[d] the principle of collective bargaining but involve[d] some modification by which that bargaining is carried out'.[30]

The details of what was referred to as the 'Wages Advisory Council' were worked out in the latter months of 1950. In its final manifestation the council could be described as a tripartite body of honest brokers, employers and union leaders. It was to provide advice on all collective negotiations on rates of remuneration, taking into account a periodically announced definition of what the government considered to be an average wage increase commensurate with the national interest. The council would publish opinions as to whether a particular claimant deserved more or less than the pre-announced national average, bearing in mind labour demand and supply and social justice. Voluntary collective negotiation, it was emphasized, was to remain an essential part of our democratic way of life and no resort to compulsion was envisaged.[31]

Gaitskell and Bevan (now at the Ministry of Labour) put the 'Wages Advisory Council' to trade union representatives in February 1951.[32] Bevan assured Gaitskell that as he was on good terms with all the union leaders, he would be able to talk them round to the government's standpoint.[33] As it turned out Bevan's optimism was misplaced. The Chancellor reported afterwards that the TUC, while not showing a wholly irresponsible attitude, could not sanction any advisory committee, nor did it think there was any chance that formal wage restraint could be accepted without rigid price control.[34]

V
Phase V: 1951

Gaitskell had to abandon the 'Wages Advisory Council', or try to set it up without union backing. He chose the former course. Subsequently the government also dropped its plan to publish a new White Paper on 'Full Employment'. This sequel to the 1944 White Paper was to have concentrated on inflation and the new responsibilities of the public under full employment. The 'Wages Advisory Council' was to have occupied a pivotal position in the document. In the spring of 1951 the wages policy of the Attlee governments entered a fifth and final stage, in which sights were set rather lower, and short-term factors again predominated. General pleas for restraint were issued and temporary expedients investigated.

First, Gaitskell initiated investigations into a scheme to link wages directly to prices, but this plan was dismissed by the Treasury as inflationary rather than disinflationary.[35] Then over the summer he tried unsuccessfully to reach agreement with the Americans on a more sensible commodity purchasing policy which would help to stabilize import prices and hold down the cost of living. There was also discussion of a 25 per cent revaluation which would have taken 2.5 per cent off the inflation rate at a stroke. In the end, however, the only major changes in policy were a strengthening of price control and the announcement, against the wish of many Treasury officials, of the limitation of company dividends by statute. The latter was an idea which had been under discussion in Whitehall for some time, and which owed much to a memorandum submitted to the Chancellor by Nicholas Kaldor. It was hoped this departure would create the right atmosphere for wage restraint.[36]

VI
Conclusions

If we look at the theory of wage determination which underlay the various phases of wages policy in the years 1945–51, we can pick out elements of thought consistent with both the wartime and prewar discussions and more recent utterances on the subject. No exact relationship between aggregate demand and wage inflation was put forward. The new peacetime conditions of full employment were merely seen as being conducive to both demand-pull and cost-push inflation. High levels of demand and employment were thought a recipe for larger and more powerful unions, which, no longer hamstrung by the fear of unemployment, or sub-subsistence income on the dole, could be expected, in the absence of eduction, to intensify their efforts to secure a high relative wage. At the same time employers were seen as being more willing to grant wage increases as they wished to attract labour and as they could pass higher costs on to consumers with less

41

fear of compromising their market share. 'Leapfrogging' was identified as a major problem, especially in view of the number of undermanned industries present early in the period. That workers would resist sharp cuts in real wages was also a central plank of the wage theory then prevalent. This was one of the reasons why the food subsidies which were such a burden on the Exchequer were retained for so long.[37]

The second point I would like to make is that in the years 1945–51 every type of wage policy from an inflation tax to a public sector wage freeze was put forward. The roots of most more recent ideas on the subject can be traced back to this period. To take just three examples, the 'Wages Advisory Council' can be seen as the precursor of the Council on Prices, Productivity and Incomes, the National Incomes Commission, the Prices and Incomes Board and the Pay Board. Statutory wage freezes became reality under Harold Wilson and Edward Heath. The idea of granting tax concessions to secure wage restraint resurfaced in the latter 1970s when Denis Healey was Chancellor.

What also becomes obvious from this survey is that the limited nature of the commitment to high and stable employment was soon replaced by a commitment to full employment that was less subject to hedges and qualifications. By February 1951 the government had informed the United Nations Economic and Social Council that a level of unemployment of 3 per cent was the maximum it would tolerate and that action to maintain full employment would be initiated well before that level was reached.[38] It was, however, never really a viable proposition to limit properly the commitment to full employment at this time. To have removed all the excess purchasing power from the economy would have severely retarded Britain's industrial regeneration, put paid to the welfare state, drastically reduced Labour's chances of re-election and conjured up the spectre of 1931. As James Meade put it in 1946,

in present circumstances it is impracticable to take such extensive action as immediately to remove the general excess of potential demand.[39]

Moreover, the need to rearm for the Korean War further lengthened the period in which a limited commitment was not possible.

As can be seen from Figure 4.1, despite the natural run-down in government expenditure after the war and the disinflation policies initiated by Dalton and consolidated by Cripps, excess demand was by no means eradicated prior to rearmament for Korea, which began in

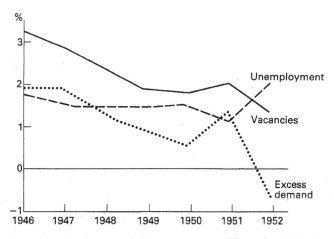

Figure 4.1 *Excess Demand, Unemployment and Vacancies, 1946–52*

Note: Excess demand is roughly twice the difference between vacancies (%) and unemployment (%).
Source: J. C. R. Dow and L. Dicks-Mireaux, 'The excess demand for labour', *Oxford Economic Papers*, n. s., vol. x, pp. 1–33.

the summer of 1950.[40] Thus the Labour government came to use wages policy as an adjunct to its demand-management policy, in a similar manner to its price subsidy and production policies. That is to say, it was used to help to compensate for the absence of balance between aggregate demand and supply, and in particular to protect the balance of payments.

How successful were the Attlee governments' wages policies? Before looking at the more obvious figures with a view to answering this question, three additional factors should be borne in mind. First, during the years 1945–51 trade union membership grew from some 7.9 million to some 9.5 million.[41] Secondly, the trade unions' bargaining position had been strengthened considerably by the Wages Councils Act of 1945. Thirdly, the movement's structure remained essentially as fragmented as ever.

However, as Figure 4.2 illustrates, wage increases fell from an average of 8–10 per cent per annum in the period June 1945–March 1948 to an average of around 3 per cent per annum for the period March 1948 to September 1949, and then to about 1.4 per cent per annum one year after devaluation. Thereafter there was a sizeable

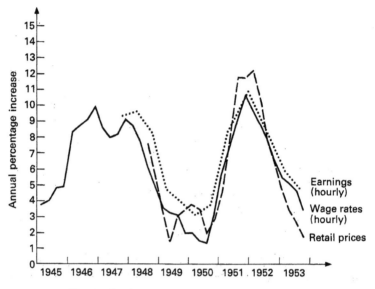

Figure 4.2   *Wages, Earnings and Prices, 1945–53*

Source: Calculated from Department of Employment and Productivity, *British Labour Statistics, Historical Abstract 1886–1968* (London: HMSO, 1971), Tables 27, 85 and 91.

jump to a rate of some 11 per cent per annum as the Korean War made its presence felt. Retail prices increased by an average of about 4 per cent from mid 1948 to devaluation, with an initial sharp fall from 7.5 per cent to 1.5 per cent. In the year after devaluation they increased by around 3 per cent, before they too exploded in 1951. Real wages, therefore, remained stationary, or indeed fell, over the period March 1948 to autumn 1950, the period when wages policy can be said to be in operation. If we look at earnings, which in fact are a better guide to remuneration over this period, especially as hours of work fell, we see a similar pattern emerge to that of wage movements, though real earnings grew considerably to mid 1951. Turning next to unemployment, the rate in the period 1948–50 oscillated around 300,000, implying that between March 1948 and the end of 1950 wages grew no faster than in the mid 1930s, when unemployment was five or six times greater. Finally, if we look again at wage inflation before the 1948 White Paper and take into account the enormous excess demand in the

44

Table 4.1 *Annual Rates of Inflation 1946–51 (per cent)*

	1946	1947	1948	1949	1950	1951
UK	1.3	5.8	6.7	2.9	2.8	8.2
Austria	26.2	97.2	45.5	31.6	10.3	27.6
Belgium	−4.9	2.1	14.7	−3.1	0.5	9.4
Canada	−3.11	14.7	12.8	8.4	3.9	11.1
Denmark	−0.6	3.1	2.4	0.6	4.1	10.0
France	–	–	–	18.1	10.4	17.4
Eire	−1.2	5.8	2.8	1.1	0.5	7.8
Italy	18.0	62.4	5.7	1.7	−2.0	9.0
Japan	–	–	72.9	–	−7.5	15.1
Holland	16.0	7.4	5.4	1.9	10.1	9.6
Switzerland	−0.7	4.6	3.1	−1.2	−1.9	4.3
USA	8.8	14.0	7.7	−1.1	0.6	7.9
W. Germany	–	–	–	–	−5.7	8.8

Calculated from IMF *International Financial Statistics* (New York: IMF).

economy, the fact that import prices rose between 1945–7 by some 30 per cent (as opposed to 15 per cent in 1947–9), and the effect of demobilization on the structure of wage rates and earnings, it is not absurd to suggest that the trade unions exerted moderation before 1948 too, as indeed they themselves claimed.[42]

These statistics imply that the Attlee governments' wages policy enjoyed a considerable degree of success in difficult circumstances, especially in the years 1948–50. Whether or not this period represents the most successful example of wage restraint in the postwar era is, however, a leading question. After all the formal policy lasted only two and a half years – spring 1948 to autumn 1950 – and as such enjoyed a similar effective lifespan to more recent policies. What can be said for certain is that the wage restraint was important in ensuring that British inflation was by no means excessive in comparison with our major competitors (as Table 4.1 indicates) and that full employment exerted less of a strain on our balance of payments than might have been expected.

What reasons lay behind the short-term success of the Attlee governments' wages policy? Perhaps the most obvious explanation lies in the moderation and support given for wage restraint by senior union leaders such as Vincent Tewson, Arthur Deakin, Tom Williamson and Will Lawther.[43] These men enjoyed a close rapport with both ministers and officials. In addition to the normal links between the unions and the

Labour Party, the extension of the wartime arrangements for consultation with industry drew them further into the policy-making process
and made them feel they had an important role to play.[44] A second
reason was the moral influence of Cripps and Bevin. Cripps could put
the case for austerity better than anybody before or since, while Bevin
was still seen by the rank and file as the trade unionists' personal
representative in Cabinet. It is perhaps worth noting that wage
restraint really broke down when ill health had forced both men to
retire from the front line.[45] We should also remember that Labour put
into operation many policies close to the heart of trade unionists. The
government nationalized the commanding heights of the economy,
presided over full employment, introduced a National Health Service
and other welfare provisions and repealed the hated Trades Disputes
Act of 1927.

While the short-term success of Labour's wages policies is not in
doubt, this success should not be allowed to cloud the development of
certain ominous long-term implications for full employment and
counter-inflation policies in the immediate postwar era. This period
witnessed a notable growth in 'wage drift', or payment by results, and
company and plant bargaining. The Attlee governments did nothing of
substance to come to terms with these developments, which were to
have profound significance for future wages policies. In particular, the
successful control of national wage rates did not necessarily mean a
successful counter-inflation policy. Furthermore, when Labour left
office, despite the existence of a moderate leadership in the trade union
movement, wages policy had helped to leave the fabric of government–
union relations in some disarray. The institutions and traditions of
British industrial relations provided no basis for a moderate General
Council to stop affiliated unions from maximizing their bargaining power
when they wanted to. In 1946 Sir Walter Citrine, then General
Secretary, described the TUC as 'the Parliament of Labour', and added
that its authority was 'not only unchallenged, but unchallengeable'.[46]
He was proved absolutely wrong within five years. George
Woodcock's oft-repeated warning in later years that it was dangerous
to treat the union movement as an army with a definite pyramid of
command was proved more apt. Restraint imposed from above could
last for a limited period only.

Traditionally the trade unions had been on the defensive, and took
whatever they could obtain from collective bargaining. This was a habit
that in the absence of structural, constitutional and philosophical

re-evaluation, could only be suspended for a limited period. This lesson proved rather traumatic for the moderate trade union leaders and was a black warning for future governments: a warning that was too readily ignored, or glossed over, as we shall see.

5

Thirteen Years of Tory Economic Policy

I
External Crisis 1951–2

In the general election of October 1951 the Conservatives under Churchill were returned to power with a small majority. While the Tories were keen to live down their reputation of the 1930s as the party of unemployment, they were also committed to the dismantling of controls and the freeing of the economy from what they saw as the rigidities and bureaucracy of Labour rule. Moreover, Churchill was anxious to cast off the stigma of his actions during the General Strike of 1926 and to pursue a policy of industrial conciliation and appeasement. Thus the Tories wanted to maintain full employment if the external account would allow it, but were reluctant to use direct controls and to embroil themselves in any labour market intervention which might result in costly strikes and industrial disputes.

On coming to power the new government faced a serious balance of payments crisis resulting from the rapid rise in the volume and price of imports wrought by western rearmament for the Korean War, and the reduction in net invisible income caused by the seizure of the Abadan oil refinery in Persia. The principal action taken to deal with the rapidly escalating deficit was, ironically, to cut imports by using direct controls, but it was also obvious to policy-makers that financial measures were needed to reduce the pressure of demand and to restore foreign confidence in sterling. In the fourth quarter of 1951 prices were rising at an annual rate of 21.1 per cent and wages at an annual rate of 11 per cent.

Treasury officials and the Bank of England pressed for severe cuts in public expenditure, a rescheduling of the rearmament programme and a reactivation of monetary policy, which had not been used for stabilization purposes by Labour. Robert Hall, the Director of the Economic Section, agreed that perhaps the economy was being run at too high a pressure of demand, but was not convinced that traditional deflationary action could remove all the pressure for wage increases without going to extremes and creating massive unemployment. This he saw as 'economically wrong as well as politically disastrous'.[1] He told Sir Edward Bridges:

Experience suggests that very high levels of unemployment indeed are necessary to put a really effective stop on wage increases . . . no Government in the U.K. would be likely to push unemployment as far as this . . .
  It must be accepted, therefore, that practicable levels of unemployment will still leave workers in so strong a bargaining position that there is always a danger of wage increases going further than is consistent with price stability.[2]

Hall proposed therefore that the government should also respond to the crisis by the publication of a White Paper giving a brief discussion of the problems of full employment in relation to the balance of payments, the movement of labour between industries and the wage–price spiral, and outlining the choice between unemployment, steady cost inflation and a permanent policy of wage moderation. He concluded optimistically:

It seems very likely that if the choice were placed squarely before the country, they would choose moderation rather than either unemployment or rapidly rising prices.[3]

In December several drafts were prepared by the Economic Section and the Treasury's Economic Information Division which made clear that it was impossible to combine full employment, free collective bargaining and price stability without workers exercising restraint. When these came to be viewed by the Ministry of Labour, officials made clear their belief that such an approach would be 'doomed from the start' because the public would take it as an indication that the government was finding excuses to attack full employment policy. As a result, subsequently a different approach was taken, and by the end of January, to the disappointment of Hall, Bridges and Plowden, the draft White Paper had been transformed into something beginning to show a resemblance to the White Paper of 1948.[4] As it turned out, however, this form of statement was not to see the light of day either, because eventually R. A. Butler, the Chancellor, decided against the release of any White Paper at all.[5]

49

Instead the government raised bank rate to 4 per cent, increased profits tax, and despite it adverse effect on price expectations, cut food subsidies by £160 million. In his regular meetings with trade union leaders Butler urged moderation in wage bargaining and asked them to investigate ways to keep the national wage bill in step with productivity growth. But the TUC Economic Committee was reluctant to recommend anything other than generally responsible collective bargaining to the rank and file in the absence of a more sympathetic government policy on prices, and for fear of a rebuff from Congress.[6]

During 1952 and 1953, with the aid of a sizeable counter-swing in commodity prices the external account recovered rapidly and inflationary pressure abated. The rate of increase in prices declined steadily to around 1 per cent per annum by the beginning of 1954, and the rate of increase in basic weekly wage rates fell to 3.6 per cent in the last quarter of 1953. By the spring of 1954 output, encouraged by an expansionary budget in 1953, was growing steadily, wages were rising by not much more than productivity, prices were more or less stable and the current account was in surplus.

II
The Economic Implications of Full Employment and the 'Price Plateau'

Despite this seemingly satisfactory picture, there were worries at this time about the growing habit of seeking and expecting an annual wage increase. The upward drift in wage rates was being described by officials as 'the great unsolved economic problem of the post-war years'.[7] The question of the wages problem was brought to a head at this particular juncture by the Morris Court of Enquiry into engineering workers' wages, which recommended that an analysis be made by an independent *ad hoc* authoritative body, of the various general economic issues apt to be raised by particular wage claims. When this idea was put to the TUC by the Minister of Labour, he found the Congress 'unalterably opposed' to it.[8] However, acting on the advice of Sir Vincent Tewson, the General Secretary of the TUC, the Ministry of Labour suggested that as an alternative, the government might issue a White Paper (if possible to be agreed with the NJAC), similar to that suggested by Robert Hall late in 1951. It was believed by the Ministry of Labour that a period of relatively stable prices would be an opportune moment to release such a document, as it might help to pre-empt any re-escalation of the wage–price spiral. Ministry of Labour officials drafted an initial synopsis of a White Paper, but this was dismissed by the Treasury as 'too diffuse in theme and unlikely to carry conviction'. Clem Leslie, Head of the Treasury's Economic Information Division, with the aid of the now knighted Robert Hall and the Economic Section and the Central Statistical Office (CSO), drafted an alternative version, which met with Ministry of Labour approval. [9]

Leslie's 19-page draft began by noting how full employment had now become institutionalized and it emphasized how the conditions of 'reasonable stability' in wages and prices and of adequate exports mentioned in the 1944 White Paper on *Employment Policy* were still valid. It then went on to decribe in detail how home costs, and labour costs in particular, had been the most important influences on prices in the period since the war, and how in a highly competitive international environment, Britain could not afford excessive inflation. The document then echoed the core of the Labour government's 1948 White Paper in noting how 'the principle of collective bargaining, unfettered from the outside, is the foundation of industrial relations [in Britain], questioned by neither party in industry, nor any party in state'. Finally, the draft outlined the action the government should take to tackle the wages problem in 1954. First, it should actively involve itself in any international action to stabilize commodity prices. Secondly, it should endeavour to provide a competitive environment to penalize excessive cost and price increases. This would be underpinned by balanced demand management policies. Thirdly, it should emphasize that:

it is the duty of Government to ensure that the problem in its full significance and gravity is understood throughout the country. This is the best means of ensuring that the collective wisdom and restraint of the Community will furnish in practice the remedies which no administrative formula . . . can provide.

Thus it was stressed that workers should try to offer productivity improvements to match any wage increase and that firms should try to meet increased costs by raising efficiency as much as possible. The draft concluded:

Full employment without price stability in a nation which lives by overseas trade is a long-term impossibility, but if the collective wisdom, moderation and good sense of employers and trade unionists, enlightened by a clear awareness of the issues at stake, can be brought to bear upon the problem, it will be solved. [10]

By the beginning of July, however, it became clear, to the chagrin of Sir Robert Hall, that Reginald Maudling, the Economic Secretary to the Treasury, was by no means convinced of the desirability of such a White Paper. He instructed the Chancellor that he thought Leslie's draft contained too much exhortation, which 'by itself . . . may do more harm than good', and was too detailed and 'too much in the nature of a learned treatise' where it gave information. If any White Paper was to be published, Maudling wanted it to be much briefer and confined to explaining in simple terms the basic message that domestic costs tended to rise faster than imported costs, and that costs in the UK tended to rise faster than in our competitors' economies. Butler, obviously not too concerned whether a White Paper was published or not, scrawled a comment to Maudling which read, 'Is it worth trying your hand at a light "fugue"? If so, I will get out my violin. Otherwise I think settle for oblivion.'[11]

Maudling did indeed produce his own shorter and more factual draft, which Butler described as 'an advance' over Leslie's version.[12] However, the Chancellor then became worried that if a White Paper of this kind was published at that stage, both Parliament and public would be led to believe that there was a crisis in the offing, which in reality did not exist. As a result the White Paper was shelved, although not completely abandoned. The government intended to keep the matter of its publication under consideration, while in the mean time the Minister of Labour made a full statement to the NJAC on the subject of the government's thinking on wages, prices and full employment. This, it was hoped, would be reported widely in the press in such a way as to render the publication of a White Paper unnecessary, while at the same time avoiding a panic.[13]

In 1955 the economy became rather overheated. Spurred on by a 'give-away' pre-election budget, and boom conditions in Europe and the USA, British unemployment hit a postwar low of 228,000 towards the end of the year. Wages were growing by some 7 per cent per annum, earnings by around 9 per cent per annum, and price inflation rose to 6 per cent. Sterling came under severe pressure. The government responded with some deflationary measures, but Harold Macmillan, the new Chancellor, was extremely reluctant to add to the dole queues to achieve a reduction in inflation. He launched an alternative policy for price stability.

The first part of Macmillan's strategy was to publish the White Paper which Sir Robert Hall had been so keen to release for the previous five years. *The Economic Implications of Full Employment,*[14] drafted in the main by Dick Ross of the Economic Section and Burke Trend, then working for Butler at the Lord Privy Seal's office, was published in March 1956.[15] It covered much the same ground as the unpublished Treasury draft of the summer of 1954. It outlined how wage and price inflation was an obvious social evil, and that it could also lead Britain, a country which lived by trading, to price itself out of export markets. It went on to describe how, while governments could contribute to forcing up prices by pursuing over-expansionary economic policies, prices could also be forced up by pressure for higher incomes, even when the level of demand was not particularly excessive.

In order to maintain full employment the Government must ensure that the level of demand for goods and services is high and rises steadily as productive capacity grows. This means a strong demand for labour, and good opportunities to sell goods and services profitably. In these conditions, it is open to employees to insist on large wage increases, and it is possible for employers to grant them and pass the cost to the consumer, so maintaining their profit margin. This is the danger which confronts the country. If the prosperous economic conditions necessary to maintain full employment are exploited . . . price stability and full employment become incompatible.[16]

The White Paper's conclusion was that the solution lay in self-restraint in making wage claims and fixing profit margins and prices, and in greater productivity. The government could not provide the whole answer to inflation in the context of full employment.

The second part of Macmillan's strategy was to appeal in May to the business community for a temporary 'price plateau' and to institute a price freeze in the public sector. The Prime Minister, Sir Anthony Eden, then sought to use his negotiating skills to secure trade union agreement to a consistent wage freeze to break the wage–price spiral. But while relations with the unions were outwardly cordial enough considering the political complexion of the government, and serious consideration was given to the proposal by the TUC General Council, it was eventually turned down, ostensibly on the grounds that the government would not reintroduce food subsidies. The General Council would go no further than to issue a warning against a wages free-for-all. One must question, however, whether even if the General Council had accepted the proposal, the rank and file would have toed the line. At the 1956 Annual TUC Conference a resolution was passed supporting 'the right of labour to bargain on equal terms with capital, and to use its bargaining strength to protect the workers from the dislocations of an unplanned economy', and which rejected 'proposals to recover control [of the economy] by wage restraint'. The passage of this resolution reflected to an extent a leftward shift in the political balance of the union movement, amply illustrated by the replacement of the deceased moderate TGWU leader Arthur Deakin by the militant Frank Cousins.

III
Thorneycroft and the 'Three Wise Men'

Any hopes for the 'price plateau' soon evaporated as the Suez Crisis broke, leading to increases in fuel and transport prices, and Sir Robert Hall was convinced that not nearly enough ministerial support was forthcoming to back up the message of the White Paper. By early 1957 the government was again in search of a way to strengthen the country's defences against wage and price inflation. Peter Thorneycroft succeeded Harold Macmillan as Chancellor in January of that year when the latter became Prime Minister. Initially, like his predecessor, he was reluctant to use deflation and unemployment to cure inflation. Instead he wanted to introduce an explicit 'guiding light' for wage claims, as suggested by Sir Robert Hall. Cabinet rejected this proposal as it was too interventionist and as any maximum figure for pay settlements might soon come to be regarded as a minimum by negotiators. However, in July 1957 ministers did approve as an alternative the creation of the Council on Prices, Productivity and Incomes, or the 'Three Wise Men' as it became known. The council consisted of three independent members – initially Lord Cohen, a law lord; Sir Harold Hewitt, a pillar of the accountancy profession; and the wartime Treasury adviser and Cambridge economist, Sir Denis Robertson. The economists Bryan Hopkin and Frank Blackaby formed the secretariat. Its terms of reference were wide-ranging and were to have

regard to the desirability of full employment and increasing standards of life based on expanding production and reasonable stability in prices and the level of incomes (including wages, salaries and profits) and to report thereon.[17]

Ostensibly the council very much fitted in with the recommendation of the 1954 Morris Court of Inquiry into the engineering dispute for the setting-up of an authoritative and impartial body to give guidance on general issues that should govern wage settlements. It was not to concern itself with individual wage claims or disputes, but as Thorney-croft told the House of Commons, 'our hope is that [the Council] will create a further appreciation of the facts, both in the public at large, and amongst those more immediately concerned with price and cost matters'.[18]

In September 1957 another sterling crisis developed, and although wage and price inflation was much lower than the previous year's peak, Thorneycroft saw rising prices as the major reason for the loss of foreign confidence. Influenced by the Governor of the Bank of England (Lord Cobbold), the Head of Overseas Finance at the Treasury (Sir Leslie Rowan), his two junior ministers Enoch Powell and Nigel Birch, and Professor Lionel Robbins, upon whom he called for additional advice, he decided that the solution lay in deflation and less expan-sionary demand-management policies. Moreover, he indicated that he favoured a greater emphasis on the control of the money supply and making price stability the major priority in economic policy in future. Bank rate was raised by 2 per cent to 7 per cent, a ceiling on advances was imposed and cuts were made in public investment projects. Thorneycroft's new stance was anathema to Sir Roger Makins, the Permanent Secretary to the Treasury, and to many Treasury econo-mists, and also had many critics in Cabinet, not least of them the Prime Minister. Sir Robert Hall, whose relations with the Governor of the Bank of England were, to say the least, strained, even considered resignation over the matter. He remained convinced that deflation could not solve the wages problem unless it was taken to destructive extremes and he predicted that this particular deflationary package would only exacerbate an economic downturn already on its way. He had little time for Thorneycroft's monetarism either.[19]

Thorneycroft and his Treasury team resigned *en masse* in January 1958 when the Cabinet, worried by rising unemployment and industrial stagnation sought to allow public expenditure to rise by £50 million rather than be pegged to the previous autumn's ceiling. The next month saw the publication of the first report of the Council on Prices, Productivity and Incomes. Although this drew on written and oral evidence submitted by all the major economic institutions and a number of academic economists, it was dominated by Sir Denis Robertson's views. Lord Cohen did not have the economic know-how to argue with Robertson and Hewitt was unwilling to do so. Only Hopkins and Blackaby seriously questioned his analysis, but as the secretariat their opinions were not considered to be of primary importance. Robertson was a conservative economist who had split with Keynes and his followers over *The General Theory* and still bore the scars of this academic conflict. He wanted publicly to assault the sacred cow of the full employment commitment and did so in the report. The 'September measures' were described as 'justified and overdue' and the mainspring of inflation seen as 'an abnormally high level of demand for an abnormally long stretch of time'. The report's conclusion was that rather than a 'guiding light' being introduced for wages in future, the economy should be run at a higher level of unemployment, more note should be taken of monetary growth and the commitment to full employment should be diluted.

The report provoked an indignant reaction from many economists and politicians, particularly those on the left. The TUC for its part was so shocked by the negative and abrasive tone of the report that it declared it would have no more dealings with the council. The so-called 'Wise Men' had contrived to produce a hostile, uncooperative response from the trade unions, when for protracted moderation in wage bargaining the opposite was required.

IV

'Pay Pause' 1961

Derek Heathcoat Amory succeeded Thorneycroft as Chancellor. He began cautiously, continuing Thorneycroft's emphasis on curing inflation and building up the reserves, although with rather less missionary zeal than his predecessor. The external account recovered as wage and price inflation moderated throughout 1958 and the economy dipped into recession. By the end of the year unemployment had risen above half a million for the first time since the fuel crisis of 1947. Encouraged by Macmillan, Amory responded to this by introducing an extremely generous pre-election budget in 1959 which offered major tax concessions across the board. This took its time to work through into wages and prices – they were more or less stable for much of 1959, but a year later it became obvious that Amory's budget had added considerable momentum to an upswing that was already under way, with all too familiar repercussions for inflation and import demand. Macmillan persuaded Amory to temper his deflationary inclinations in April 1960, but by July 1961, when Selwyn Lloyd had replaced Amory as Chancellor, a major sterling crisis demanded drastic action.

Sir Robert Hall was pushing for the introduction of a 'guiding light' for wages throughout this period. He saw a time of stable or near-stable prices as a wonderful opportunity to secure trade union co-operation in adhering to this. Ministers, however, took a very different view, as they had in 1954. They questioned why they should become embroiled in potentially politically destabilizing discussions with the unions at a time when they did not really need their support.[20] The later 1950s also saw the 'Phillips Curve gain some credence in Whitehall. An article by A. W. Phillips of the London School of Economics published in 1958 put forward the hypothesis, already hinted at by the Council on Productivity, Prices and Incomes, that the rate of change of money-wages and hence prices could be accurately explained by the level of unemployment. As the economy moved below an unemployment level of 5 per cent, the rate of increase in money-wages would escalate rapidly, particularly once it moved below 2 per cent. The implication was that by running the economy at slightly higher levels of unemployment than the 1.5 per cent average of the postwar period, inflation could be reduced to negligible proportions and a 'guiding light' or indeed any incomes policy rendered unnecessary.[21]

Sir Robert Hall campaigned for a more interventionist approach in the labour market for all of his fourteen years as Director of the Economic Section and Chief Economic Adviser. It was, however, only after he had retired from this post, to be replaced by Professor Sir Alec Cairncross, that opinion changed sufficiently in Whitehall for the Conservative government to introduce a formal incomes policy. In response to the sterling crisis of July 1961, and in addition to standard deflationary measures, Selwyn Lloyd announced an indefinite 'wage pause' for government employees, which was later extended to workers covered by wages councils, and which it was hoped would set an example to private sector employers. Commitments already entered into were, however, to be honoured. The policy lasted for nine months, and despite trade union antipathy, it probably shocked people into an awareness of the wages problem which the intermittent exhortations of the previous decade had not done. The inflation of basic weekly wage rates moderated from in excess of 4 per cent per annum in the first half of 1961 to 2.8 per cent in the first quarter of 1962. It is hard, however, to gauge exactly what role the 'wage pause' played in this as unemployment was rising fairly steeply at the time too. What can be said for certain is that the public sector suffered considerably more under this policy than the private sector.

The conversion to incomes policy in 1961 emanated from several sources. It was partially the result of the need to deal firmly and rapidly with a sterling crisis. It reflected too the fact that the new Permanent Secretary to the Ministry of Labour, Sir Lawrence Helsby, a former economics don and Treasury official, saw his role much less in terms of conciliation than his predecessors. But the switch was also the result of theoretical considerations. The Fourth Report of the Council on Productivity, Prices and Incomes appeared in July 1961. It was drafted by three new 'wise men', including Professor Henry Phelps Brown, the Keynesian Labour economist, and Sir Harold Emmerson, a former senior Ministry of Labour official. Their report embodied a major shift in attitude to the wages problem back towards the position taken by Sir Robert Hall. It emphasized that

experience has shown that removing excess demand was not of itself enough ... inflation has another cause, an upward push as rates of pay are raised and profit margins are maintained by rising prices.

It added that 'today' wages had 'a capacity for self-propulsion which restraint of demand by itself seems unlikely to hold back without creating heavy unemployment'.[22] Furthermore, between the budget of 1961 and the July sterling crisis, a report of the Organization for European Economic Co-operation (OEEC) on *The Problem of Rising Prices* was published which added support to the 'cost-push' theory of inflation, and convinced many Treasury officials that the wages problem should be tackled by direct action as well as by financial policies.[23] In an article published shortly after his retirement, Sir Robert Hall commented:

With the passage of time the number of adherents of extreme positions has diminished and a large body of opinion now thinks that some form of wage policy other than leaving wages to free collective bargaining is necessary if full employment and stable prices are to be combined. In this connection, the OEEC Report on the problem of rising prices is extremely significant since it is very nearly an agreed document, by highly respected economists from a number of western countries who can certainly not be regarded as all belonging to any particular school of thought.[24]

V
The 'Guiding Light', 'Nicky' and 'Neddy'

In announcing the 'pay pause' Selwyn Lloyd also pledged that the government would endeavour to 'work out a sensible long-term relationship between increases in incomes of all sorts and increases in productivity'.[25] But on arriving in Whitehall from Glasgow University (which as much as any university in Britain at that time specialized in labour market economics), Professor Cairncross had been amazed at the ignorance he encountered, not just in the Treasury, but in the Ministry of Labour, on the subject of pay determination and the processes of collective bargaining. It was obvious that in working out this long-term policy officials would have to start from scratch. Furthermore, when Cairncross went to the TUC to discuss future policy with the General Secretary, George Woodcock, he found him angry and dismayed that the government should seek his advice on this matter after the announcement of the incomes policy rather than before, and as they had done nothing to sweeten the bitter pill of a wage freeze. Woodcock could offer little solace. He was not confident that any formula for limiting wage inflation to the growth of productivity could be successfully imposed from above and doubted his ability to control the rank and file for more than six months.[26]

The government's follow-up policy was finally made public in February 1962. A White Paper entitled *National Incomes Policy: The Next Step*[27] set a 'guiding light' for money income growth of 2.5 per cent per person per annum to match the average growth of productivity in the 1950s. The White Paper went on to indicate a number of criteria which should be taken into account by wage negotiators in framing their wage claims. These were remarkably similar to those outlined in the 1948 *Statement on Personal Incomes, Costs and Prices*. Higher productivity could justify a wage increase where 'those concerned made a direct contribution by accepting more exacting work, or more onerous conditions, or by a renunciation of restrictive practices'. Arguments derived from increases in the cost of living or from the trends of profits or productivity in a particular industry could not in themselves be regarded as providing a sound basis for an increase. Claims for increases based on the need to attract labour to an undermanned industry should be permitted only where they were absolutely necessary. It was pointed out that criteria which had in the past been used to justify higher wages and salaries such as comparability 'ought not to be given the same weight as hitherto'. The White Paper focused on earnings and contained nothing specific, either on prices or profits, or in terms of proposals to deal with the problem of wage drift, it was merely emphasized that:

> In considering increases in wages and salaries what matters for costs and prices is not simply the change in rates, but the amount actually paid. It will therefore be necessary to have regard to the likelihood judged from past experience, that basic rates will in practice be supplemented in certain employments by local or special payments. Changes in pay made under particular agreements (e.g. related to the cost of living) and reductions in hours or similar improvements will also have to be included in the reckoning.

There is no doubt that both officials and ministers had a lot of trouble deciding the exact format that wages policy should take after the pause. The White Paper was drafted time and again before an acceptable version was found and its rather tentative and uncertain style mirrors the fact that it represented the maximum which could be agreed upon when many remained convinced too much intervention was a bad thing, but several parties wanted extensively to modify the collective bargaining process. Macmillan for one was convinced of the need for permanent intervention in the labour market and favoured the creation of a new institution to help decide, without compulsion, priorities among different kinds of workers and different kinds of income.[28] Some officials wanted to find a better way to introduce national economic considerations into the actual process of negotiation, while others wanted to condemn in public wage settlements which were against the national interest, as soon as they were announced.

The failure of the Treasury and the rather inarticulate Selwyn Lloyd to come up with acceptable new institutional arrangements to back the 'guiding light' policy at a time when Macmillan was looking to reflate the economy in anticipation of the next election, eventually led to the Prime Minister's taking the initiative himself and, indeed, to the Chancellor's dismissal. Macmillan assembled a group of officials including Sir Lawrence Helsby and threshed out a plan to set up a National Incomes Commission (or 'Nicky' as it became known). This was announced to the public on 26 July 1962. The body was composed of independent members and chaired by Sir Geoffrey Lawrence, QC. Its limited terms of reference were to review matters relating to pay where the cost was wholly or partially met from the exchequer if the government asked it to do so, and to examine retrospectively any particular pay settlement which the government referred to it. It was not to concern itself with pricing or profit policies. 'Nicky' flouted the convention that collective bargaining was the sole responsibility of unions and employers and led the government to involve itself in specific bargains. The TUC strongly objected to the notion that 'some group of independent people, some outsiders, [could] take on their shoulders the burden of defining what was the national interest for one section of the community – the wage earners'.[29] As a result by the time 'Nicky' had become operative in November 1962 it was already a dead letter – the trade unions would have nothing to do with its recommendations.

Between the summer of 1962 and the spring of 1963 the government took action to reflate the economy. It was anxious to hit the target rate of growth of 4 per cent put up by the National Economic Development Council (the NEDC, or 'Neddy' as it became known), especially after the disappointing economic performance of 1961 and 1962. In March 1963 'Nicky', on the advice of the influential National Institute for Economic and Social Research, announced that the 'guiding light' had been increased to what was in this expansionary context a more realistic level of 3–3.5 per cent. This, as it transpired, was to be 'Nicky's' only major effect on policy. All in all it produced five reports on four references, and these were published too long after the wage agreements had been concluded to have a major impact on public opinion. In 1963 and 1964 the NEDC became the major focus for wages policy.

The NEDC was set up after the sterling crisis of 1961 in response to general impatience with Britain's structural deficiencies and poor economic performance relative to its major competitors. It was in effect a national planning council serviced by its own independent officials in the National Economic Development Office and involving representatives of government and both sides of industry with the Chancellor serving as chairman. Early in its existence 'Neddy' became committed to a 4 per cent annual growth rate and the end of the 'stop–go' cycle of the 1950s. It was also always hoped by officials and ministers that 'Neddy' could be used as a forum in which the unions could be made more aware of their responsibilities with regard to wage moderation. In fact the unions originally only agreed to sit on the council if they received assurances that it would not be used as an incomes policy 'trap'. By early 1963, however, wages were being openly discussed and a report was drafted with the consent of the trade union representatives which noted that in the context of a planned economic expansion there was a need for wage restraint. Thereafter paper after paper discussed by the NEDC embodied this conclusion, and potential means to achieve this restraint were examined.

Reginald Maudling, who took over from Selwyn Lloyd as Chancellor in the summer of 1962, was expansion-minded and, in sharp contrast to his position eight years before, very keen to obtain agreement to a joint statement from unions and employers urging responsibility on all sides within the context of the 'guiding light' for wages. His 1963 budget was drawn up with the need to win union support for an incomes policy in mind. The across-the-board tax cuts he announced amounted to a wage increase of 2 per cent for many workers. Although Maudling managed to obtain the employers' acceptance of a new price review body, and although he convinced the trade unions' representatives to recognize that restraints on profits could not be as tight as on wages, he was unsuccessful. The trade union leadership was understandably reluctant to offer the Conservatives a major political coup in the run-up to the next general election. Furthermore, it could claim that it had no real mandate to discuss wage restraint with the government, as the 1963 TUC Conference voted to oppose its imposition in any form. By the summer of 1964 officials no longer bothered to pretend that an incomes policy of any sort existed.

If we look at the course of inflation after the initial announcement of the 'guiding light', we see that the growth of wages fell from an annual rate of 4.2 per cent in mid 1962 to 3.5 per cent at the end of 1963. It was only in 1964 that wage inflation accelerated as the economy overheated in response to the government's expansionary policies. Prices showed a similar pattern. Price inflation fell from a peak of 5.6 per cent in mid 1962 to as low as 1.3 per cent in mid 1963, before accelerating to 4.5 per cent in the third quarter of 1964. Thus, for much of the period 1962–4, the revised 'guiding light' was more or less observed. Once again, however, that this was solely the direct result of observance of the government's guidelines is unlikely. Unemployment seems to be the most important explanatory factor.

VI
Conclusions

In the 1950s full employment became institutionalized in the UK, and successive Conservative administrations had to face up to the inflationary dangers that this brought with it. Initially, the government,

aided by a swing in terms of trade and mindful of political considerations, adopted a non-interventionist line on wages, but as external
circumstances changed somewhat, and plans to end the 'stop–go' cycle
of the 1950s were drawn up, this became less satisfactory. From the
outset the Chief Economic Adviser, Sir Robert Hall, was anxious for a
more active approach on the wages front to underpin demand management. He was convinced that the problem of wage inflation was here to
stay unless attitudes could be changed. This would take time and a
consistent government effort by way of propaganda, exhortation and
explanation. He was rewarded only by intermittent bursts of sympathy
and action from the government. Overall policy was never consistent in
this respect. Many of Hall's contemporaries in the Whitehall machine
did not share his views for a long time, and saw the solution in terms of
running the economy at a higher level of unemployment. In the end,
and rather ironically, Hall retired just as the bulk of official and
ministerial opinion became convinced that some modification of the
collective bargaining process was necessary. Free collective bargaining was viewed as a luxury that it could no longer afford if Britain was to
have sustained economic growth. In the years 1962–4 actually turning
this observation into an acceptable and practicable policy for wages did
not prove to be in the least bit easy.

Throughout the period 1951–64 the trade union movement was
frequently portrayed in the media as a force which had become too
strong and irresponsible. It was seen as undemocratic and extreme,
pressing constantly for high and inflationary wage settlements, breaking agreements, favouring outmoded and restrictive practices and
involving itself in petty demarcation squabbles. In short, full employment had supposedly spoiled the trade union movement. This was, of
course, a gross oversimplification. The trade union movement's
behaviour was in many ways logical and to a large extent dictated by
historical precedent and the environment it found itself in. Unions
continued to bargain as they had done in the past, when economic
conditions had not been in their favour and they had had to struggle to
get anything out of management. At a plant and company level
managers' attitudes to change were often as conservative and narrow-
minded as the unions', while at a national level there was no really
representative and powerful employers' organization to provide an
overall counterweight to a stronger union movement, or to force it into
more co-ordinated policies. The new strength of the trade union
movement under full employment emanated in the main from the shop

floor, where managers were keen to maintain production at almost any price. It was by its very nature hard to control, especially given that the British trade union movement was so fragmented in the first place. At the same time, most of the strategic aims of the interwar union movement had been achieved by the late 1940s and an aging national leadership had lost much of its collective sense of purpose and direction in the early 1950s. Thus the door was left open for maverick left-wingers on the shop floor to stir things up, and for a new breed of younger national leaders, without any experience of involvement in the policy-making process, to assert their authority. From the point of view of building up prestige and support amongst the union member-ship, negotiators at a national and local or plant level had good reason to wish to obtain high money wage settlements.

The shift of power to the shop floor expressed itself in the further extension of wage drift in the 1950s and early 1960s. The upward spiral of individual earnings at the place of work over and above national rates was increasingly making itself felt and offering a major challenge to those who wanted an incomes policy. The Conservatives did little of substance to come to terms with the problem. *The Fourth Report of the Council on Prices, Productivity and Incomes* identified the problem and called attention to two lines of policy that had been suggested to deal with it as the following extract illustrates:

One is to recognise the extent to which earnings are actually being fixed locally and the greater bargaining power on the floor of the shop that goes with this, and make constructive use of them so as to provide a more orderly wage structure. More information is needed about the nature and extent of local settlements, the other line is to increase the coverage and authority of national settlements. The two lines do not necessarily diverge: local agreements may be made on principles agreed nationally, and national agreements may be strengthened by greater liaison between the centre and the localities. It has also been suggested that some national agreements would be strengthened by a revision of the boundaries of the industries now regulated by a single negotiation ... so as to get nominally more homogeneous and manageable bargaining units.[30]

But, as we have seen, the White Paper, *Incomes Policy: The Next Step*, merely called for negotiators to look at earnings as a whole, and not just basic wage rates when bargaining collectively.

Overall, however, we must conclude that while the wages problem took up a lot of time and thought in Whitehall in the 1950s and early 1960s and could be described as a major economic difficulty of the time, it was relatively insignificant in comparison to the position in the mid

1970s, for example. Inflation had only twice gone above 5 per cent after the end of the Korean War boom and was actually negative in 1959. The exchange rate remained at $2.80 to the pound throughout and unemployment only twice rose above half a million, in 1958 and 1963. Despite Thorneycroft's rumblings in 1957 and 1958, there was never any real question of the government abandoning completely short-term stabilization policy aimed at full employment because of its inflationary impact. Nevertheless, in October 1964, when the Conservatives left office, the wage problem was no nearer solution than had been the case in 1951.

6

The Wilson Governments
1964–70

I

Voluntary Incomes Policy 1964–6

Harold Wilson's Labour Party came to power with a small overall majority in October 1964. It was faced with an economy that was booming. Unemployment had dropped sharply in February 1964 and continued to fall throughout the year: output was surging, wage increases were running at an annual rate of more than 5 per cent and the current account of the balance of payments was in considerable deficit. Towards the end of their term of office the Tories had been loath to put on the brakes with an election in the offing and while there was an antipathy amongst senior ministers towards deflation because of its association with the 'stop–go' of the 1950s. In its first months in office the new government was be faced with some difficult decisions.

For several years during its time in opposition Labour like the Tories had been committed to sustained growth and an end to 'stop–go' through the medium of 'planned economic expansion', a type of interventionist policy which, it was asserted, only a Socialist government could follow through with any degree of credibility and conviction. It has become obvious to Labour's leadership at an early stage in discussions on this type of strategy that an incomes policy would have to occupy a central role if inflation was to be constrained. Free collective bargaining as it then stood would be incompatible with expansionary policies, it had to be reformed. However, when the subject had been raised with the trade unions in the late 1950s it had not exactly been met with enthusiasm. It was hoped nevertheless that by

66

presenting incomes policy as 'planned growth of incomes' in the context of a generally expanding economy, the government might meet with a more sympathetic attitude from the TUC. Labour's leadership began to push the trade unions for co-operation in working out an incomes policy for the next Labour government in 1963. The unions leadership did indeed respond fairly favourably to the arguments that a Labour incomes policy would, in the long-run context of 'planned economic expansion', actually increase the rate of growth of real wages rather than restrain it, and would also tackle prices, profits, dividends and the distribution of income in general.

We have already noted how the TUC Annual Conference of 1963 declared 'its complete opposition to any form of wage restraint',[1] but this can be seen as a means to deny the Macmillan government a political coup at the NEDC, as much as an accurate indication of trade union feeling on the matter of wages policy as a whole. One month later the Labour Party Conference overwhelmingly passed a resolution which instructed the National Executive Committee 'to develop, in consultation with the Trade Union Movement, policies to promote sustained economic growth', an element of which was to be 'an incomes policy to include salaries, wages, dividends and profits ... and social security benefits'.[2] Even Frank Cousins, a long-time critic of wage policy, gave his support to the resolution, although he made it absolutely clear that he was supporting 'planned growth of wages' and not wage restraint, and that if the Labour government did not deliver on its planning promises, he would be quick to withdraw his support.

Delegates at the 1964 TUC Conference felt able to outline in some detail the type of wages policy they would accept. Their statement mirrored opinion at the previous year's Labour Party Conference, while describing the role they saw for themselves in the running of such a policy. Any incomes policy, it asserted

must be based on social justice, taking into account all forms of incomes, including rent, interest and profit ... Congress further believes that an acceptable incomes policy must redress the injustices in the existing wages structure, and that Congress would have to establish its own system of priorities to achieve these aims.[3]

Thus in its manifesto for the 1964 general election, the Labour Party could say,

To curb inflation we must have a planned growth of incomes so that they are broadly related to the annual growth of production. To achieve this a Labour Government will enter into urgent consultations with the unions and employers' organisations concerned ... Labour's incomes policy will not be unfairly directed at lower paid workers and public employees; instead it will apply in an expanding economy to all incomes: to profits, dividends and rents as well as to wages and salaries. [4]

The 'consultations' did indeed begin as soon as Labour came to power. Incomes policy became the responsibility of former trade union official George Brown, the Secretary of State for Economic Affairs and Deputy Prime Minister. His new department was given the job of overseeing Labour's 'economic planning' and taking over some of the responsibilities of the Treasury. At an official level at the Department of Economic Affairs (DEA), Douglas Allen and Donald MacDougall dealt with incomes policy; Allen with the mechanics, MacDougall with much of the liaising with the unions.

It was decided within a few days of the general election that devaluation was not an option the Labour government would use in trying to combine sustained economic expansion with national solvency. It would have made Labour 'the party of devaluation' and undermined sterling's role as an international currency. Incomes policy, together with a temporary import surcharge scheme and the acquisition of foreign credit, was seen as a substitute for devaluation. At the first few meetings with trade union leaders Brown immediately tried to sidestep his party's pre-election promises and introduce a temporary voluntary wage freeze with a view to bringing home to the unions the precariousness of Britain's position and to building foreign confidence in sterling. George Woodcock warned, however, that this would greatly antagonize the rank and file and destroy any hopes of introducing a long-term policy later. Thus Brown fell back on the plans for 'planned growth of incomes' and the long-term reform of the collective bargaining process. Within two months he had abolished the NIC and to his surprise already successfully persuaded the TUC and representatives of the employers' associations to sign a 'Joint Statement of Intent on Prices, Productivity and Incomes'. The statement recognized that the major economic objective was to achieve a rapid increase in output and that there was a need to keep growth in money incomes commensurate with real output to achieve price stability and to protect the balance of payments. The government promised that the DEA would prepare a 'National Plan' in consultation with the NEDC and establish machinery to monitor movements in prices and incomes, examine particular cases and help to educate public opinion. [5] Sir Donald MacDougall is convinced that this agreement could not have been concluded so rapidly or easily without the groundwork done at the NEDC in previous years. However, with an absence of major deflationary measures this voluntary incomes policy was going to have to work in the context of an increasingly tight labour market.

The National Board for Prices and Incomes (NBPI) was set up in February 1965, and in March the TUC General Council agreed to support a 3–3.5 per cent pay norm, similar to that put forward by the NIC. In April a White Paper was published which laid down criteria for both prices and incomes.[6] This document reaffirmed the pay norm of 3–3.5 per cent and outlined a number of familiar exceptions to the general rule. Above the norm pay increases were only to be permitted where employees concerned made a direct contribution towards increasing productivity; where it was essential for the national interest to secure a change in the distribution of manpower; where existing wage and salary levels were too low to maintain a reasonable standard of living; and where there was a widespread recognition that a group had fallen seriously out of line with the going rate of remuneration for similar work. These criteria were not only very similar to those used by the previous Tory administration (barring the last one), but also to those finally accepted by the trade unions in 1948, and indeed those used by John F. Kennedy's administration in the United States.

Where the White Paper did differ from previous practice was in its announcement of a further series of detailed rules for firms' pricing policy. These can be summarized as follows: if a firm's productivity was rising at a slower rate than the prospective national average, since this was to be the standard for wage increases, prices could be raised. However, if productivity was rising in excess of the national average, then for the same reasons, prices should be reduced. Where other costs rose prices could be raised if no offsetting reduction could be found elsewhere. Where other costs fell, prices should be decreased correspondingly. Finally, prices could be increased if more capital was needed for investment, but should be reduced if based on 'excessive market power'.

The members of the NBPI were drawn from both sides of the political fence and included representatives from the trade unions and employers. The chairman was an economist and former Conservative minister, Aubrey Jones. The board's job was to oversee the incomes policy by examining retrospectively individual pay settlements and pricing decisions referred to it by the government. Obviously it could only scrutinize a tiny proportion of the total number of such bargains and judgements. Its role was seen by the government as 'educative'. It was to be an instrument of long-term reform in the collective bargaining process which would work by widening understanding of the government's policy for incomes. To many trade unionists it was to represent an affront to their sovereignty no less than that of the NIC.

Why then at the end of April 1965 did the trade unions opt to accept the Labour government's incomes policy by a majority of 3:1? After all, in addition to the implications of the NBPI's role, the pay norm was half the going rate for earnings at that time and 2 per cent less than the rate of inflation. In fact, the norm of 3–3.5 per cent was accepted under protest by the TUC General Council, and then only because the government convinced it anything higher would undermine what was left of foreign confidence in sterling, and as the exceptions offered some scope for bypassing the norm. As far as supporting the policy of restraint as a whole was concerned, however, there were several reasons. The unions feared the possible alternatives of deflation and/or a statutory pay policy. They believed the government would try to deliver on growth. They were keen to maintain solidarity with the first Labour government for some thirteen years, which was at the time struggling with a tiny majority. They respected the views of TUC General Secretary George Woodcock, an Oxford-trained economist who was willing to support incomes policy as he saw it as a means by which the trade union movement could prove its responsibility and expand its role in the overall formulation of economic policy. Perhaps the most pertinent reason for its acceptance was, however, that the details of the policy were not taken too seriously. Woodcock himself warned the government that it should not expect too much and that this was only a first tentative step in the direction of planned real incomes and the reform of collective bargaining. He added that in reality there was very little chance of the growth of pay matching the government's target in the year 1965.

The voluntary incomes policy agreed to in April 1965 did not survive long. Despite a mildly deflationary budget, the labour market continued to tighten and unemployment to fall. Wage claims did not moderate and in June a speculative run on sterling developed. Rather than devalue, the government introduced a further deflationary package towards the end of July, but opinion at the US Treasury and at the IMF and the Organization for Economic Co-operation and Development (OECD) favoured in addition a tightening of incomes policy before more credit could be extended to Britain. Joe Fowler, the Secretary to the US

Treasury, told Wilson that he had no faith in the voluntary incomes policy, and urged the British Prime Minister to impose a statutory policy, preferably a 'freeze'. James Callaghan, the Chancellor of the Exchequer, concurred and Wilson himself saw the need for a tougher policy.[7]

No form of statutory intervention in the labour market was going to appeal to the trade union movement, especially after the promises made by the Labour party in opposition. George Brown had a long series of discussions with the unions before he wrested a compromise from them. The General Council eventually agreed to a voluntary system of notification and vetting of wage claims. However, the government also decided to underpin this with a Bill to give it statutory powers which it would activate via an Order in Council if the voluntary system did not work.

Under the procedure of notification and vetting for wages all unions affiliated to the TUC were expected to inform the General Council of impending claims. These were then discussed by a special 'Incomes Policy Commission' which had a month to make any comments and to call for talks with the claimants. The claimants could completely ignore its comments if they chose. The 'Incomes Policy Commission' would finally inform the Ministry of Labour about the size of the claim and offer its comments on it. Staff associations not affiliated to the TUC were expected to inform the Ministry of Labour in a similar way. The 'Incomes Policy Commission' was to continue in existence until January 1970 and in contrast to the NBPI it considered all major claims.

As far as prices were concerned, the manufacturers of some seventy-five items were asked to inform the appropriate government department not less than four weeks in advance of any proposed price increase and to give a brief justification of the increase in the light of the criteria set for price increases by the government.

These arrangements for prices and incomes were set out in another White Paper published in November 1965, entitled *Prices and Incomes: An 'Early Warning System'*,[8] and were as promised introduced initially on a non-statutory basis. The TUC backed the policy by 5.2 million to 3.3 million votes after a strong speech in favour by Woodcock. The enabling Act creating statutory powers to be held in reserve lapsed with the dissolution of Parliament in March 1966.

The 'early warning system' can hardly be described as a roaring success either. In the first six months of 1966, during which time Labour was re-elected with a greatly enlarged majority, earnings

71

inflated at an annual rate of some 10 per cent and wages were not far behind. In July unemployment was down to 1.2 per cent. The TUC's vetting committee had found its task very disconcerting and adapted a policy that was by its own admission 'flexible'. But in truth any other policy would most likely have engendered such bad blood as to have destroyed the wages policy completely. the NBPI was also encountering difficulties in fulfilling its role. The majority of settlements it dealt with exceeded the prescribed norm, and if it held back the small number of claims referred to it, its judgements were ignored. The NBPI sought a way out of this dilemma by stressing the need for productivity improvements as financial justification for above-norm settlements.

II
Statutory Freeze and
'Severe Restraint' 1966–7

Towards the end of May 1966 the National Union of Seamen called a strike over a 17 per cent pay claim. The dispute was not settled until 1 July, when a specially convened court of inquiry granted the union a 9.5 per cent increase over two years. By this time the disruption to exports caused by the strike had proved to be a major element in the developmet of yet another sterling crisis. The government's response was to bring in yet another package of deflationary fiscal and monetary measures and to enact a six-month freeze on all wages, salaries, dividends and prices, to be followed by a further period of 'severe restraint'. The object was to avoid devaluation by cutting £250 million from consumers' expenditure. The austerity measures were also to render the 'National Plan', published in September, little more than an interesting exercise in wishful thinking.

The government added a Supplementary Section to the Prices and Incomes Bill then going through Parliament to obtain statutory backing for the freeze. This Bill was a slightly revised version of the one which had lapsed in March, providing for compulsory advance notification of wage or price increases. Notification had to be given one month prior to the implementation of increases and if during that period the government decided to refer the case to the NBPI, the increase could not be granted until after the board had published a report, or three months had passed from the date of referral, whichever was earlier. The introduction of this Bill led to the resignation of Frank Cousins, who had been brought into the government as Minister of Technology. Cousins was thus free to orchestrate a campaign against the incomes policy. The supplementary portion of the Bill gave the government powers to decree that specific prices, charges, or renumeration rates be held constant from a certain date, and also to enforce the recommendations of the NBPI, although this power was never used. The use of these powers was again subject to an Order in Council and was valid for twelve months only. Genuine promotion and increases in incremental scales were the only pay increases allowed. Existing commitments on pay, which covered some 25 per cent of the workforce, could be honoured after six months. As far as prices were concerned, the only increases permissible were those resulting from seasonal factors, from the cost of imported materials, or from government action, such as increased indirect taxation.[9]

The TUC was not consulted about the freeze and found such a *fait accompli* a bitter pill to swallow. Serious consideration was given to opposing the freeze, but a threat from the government to impose more severe deflation if the unions did not toe the line led to first the General Council and then the Annual Congress offering their reluctant support. Frank Cousins and the TGWU spearheaded the opposition to the policy within the TUC. As it turned out, however, very little effort was made to break the freeze. No major negotiating body sought to defy it openly and the government's legal powers were used but sparingly, and then only to stop a wage claim agreed before the freeze was introduced. The key factor was probably that all groups knew that everybody else was being treated the same way. The rate of increase in earnings fell to about 3 per cent per annum during the freeze, and from July to December the index of weekly wage rates barely moved at all.

If the deflationary measures of July 1965 cast enormous doubts on Labour's willingness to plan for expansion to the exclusion of other considerations, the belt-tightening of July 1966 marked a definite watershed in economic policy. The rehabilitation of the external account without resort to devaluation took over from growth as the prime objective. At the same time incomes policy became much less a means to restrain domestic spending without resort to deflation, than an additional arm of deflation. Its role became inherently negative rather than positive.

While recognizing the need to avoid a wages 'free for all' in 1967, the unions were not at all keen on the idea of another round of mandatory severe restraint to follow the six-month freeze. As an alternative they

73

proposed a return to a purely voluntary policy. The General Council offered to reinstitute the system of wage review and announced that from that time on it would also publish an annual *Economic Review* which would make available information supposedly conducive to sensible wage bargaining. Furthermore, it held out the possibility of the introduction of the synchronization of major wage claims, although it refused to accept the government's request for sanctions against recalcitrant unions. When a special conference of trade union executives met to discuss this programme it was overwhelmingly approved with even the TGWU offering their support. The Prime Minister and the majority of the Cabinet, however, feared it would prove as ineffective in the short term as the last voluntary policy and instead reaffirmed their support for a statutory policy.

The policy of 'severe restraint' for January to June 1967 was detailed in a White Paper published in November. [10] This document again called for a zero norm for earnings and gave the 'early warning system' greater importance. Previously negotiated settlements would be affected by its provisions but those delayed by the previous policy could now be honoured. The major deviation from the freeze of July 1966 was that exceptions to the general rule were allowed provided they met certain criteria. Agreements for pay increases designed to improve efficiency and productivity were acceptable, although increases were not to be paid in advance. Some proven benefit to the community in the form of lower prices or increased quality was required first. Pay increases were also justifiable if they improved the standard of living of the poorest sections of the community. Certain increases might in exceptional circumstances, and after careful scrutiny, be justified on the grounds of manpower distribution. Finally, comparability claims would be considered if they sought to correct gross anomalies.

In March the government announced that a no norm incomes policy was to continue after June 1967. Another White Paper asserted that

There can be no justification at present for returning to the norm of 3–3½ per cent . . . which in practice tended to be the minimum increase which everybody expected to receive. Over the twelve-month period beginning 1 July 1967 no one can be entitled to a minimum increase; any proposed increase . . . will need to be justified against the criteria set out below.

The criteria referred to were basically the same as those set out in the 1965 White Paper, plus a few additional points. For example, twelve months were to be allowed between each claim, substantial increases were to be granted in stages and no attempt was to be made to make up for increases foregone over the previous year.[11] To enforce adherence to these criteria the government in effect returned to the provisions of the 1966 Act, which enabled it to delay an award for an NBPI examination. However, a new Bill was introduced too. A one-month standstill could be imposed while a claim was examined and a further three-month delay could be imposed if proposals were referred to the NBPI. Furthermore, at the end of three months, if the NBPI recommended it, a further delay of three months was proposed. Thus a maximum period of delay of seven months could be imposed and the NBPI became the focus of the government's delaying tactics.

This policy was largely ignored by the unions, and despite Wilson's desire for an even stronger incomes policy, little effort was made to enforce it. Indeed, its main effect was further to poison government–trade union relations. The 1967 TUC Conference passed with a large majority a resolution condemning the government's interference in the collective bargaining process and its 'Tory deflationary policies'.

III
Devaluation

The prices and incomes freeze and the period of severe restraint did not reduce inflation sufficiently to bring Britain's competitive position back into line with our main rivals. The slowdown during the freeze was followed in 1967 by an escalation in wage inflation to the pre-freeze rate, despite a sharp increase in unemployment from 1.2 per cent in July 1966 to 2.3 per cent in November 1967. This did not augur well for the balance of payments or sterling's strength. Moreover, the external account was also undermined by a neutral budget which left fiscal policy too lax and monetary growth in double figures. On top of this the depressed state of world trade in 1967 hit British exports, while imports were swollen by a number of one-off factors. Speculation against sterling was further fuelled by rumours of Britain's imminent entry into the European Economic Community (EEC), which it was thought would require devaluation. The external value of the pound, supported by inadequate reserves and overshadowed by massive short-term debts, was under continuous pressure from April 1967. A series of dock strikes in the autumn proved the straw which broke the camel's back and in mid November Wilson and Callaghan finally bowed to the inevitable and devalued by 14 per cent. A hastily assembled deflationary package was also announced and the government signed a letter of intent with regard to the achievement of certain economic targets to obtain new IMF credits.

In December further speculation against the newly devalued pound forced the government to embark on a wide-ranging review of expenditure programmes. When the cuts were made public in January 1968 they amounted to some £500 million and marked the end of Britain's pretensions to be a world power. The first budget presented by new Chancellor Roy Jenkins (Callaghan felt bound to resign after devaluation) ushered in a series of formidable tax increases and other deflationary measures designed to reduce consumers' expenditure by some 2 per cent, and keep the Public Sector Borrowing Requirement (PSBR) well below the IMF's prescribed target of £1,000 million. The government was desperate to make devaluation a success and to restore national solvency at the expense of all other policy goals. In fact it was not until the end of the year that the tide began to turn.

A new phase of incomes policy for the period to December 1969 was announced in March 1968.[12] There was still to be no norm, all increases should conform with the 1967 criteria and in addition, even within the scope provided by these criteria, there should be a ceiling of 3.5 per cent, except for agreements which would genuinely raise productivity and increase efficiency sufficiently to justify a pay increase in excess of that figure. The NBPI's guidelines for productivity agreements were restated and the government made it clear that when the relevant sections of the 1967 Act expired on 11 August 1968, it would introduce legislation to empower it to extend the deferment in pay or price increases for as long as twelve months in the context of a reference to the board. Productivity more than ever was to be the focal point for claims put forward. This fact is further illustrated by the merger of the Ministry of Labour with parts of the DEA to form a new Department of Employment and Productivity.

The unions' total antipathy to Labour's austere macroeconomic policies can be best illustrated by reference to their first *Economic Review*, which called for a resumption of 'planned expansion' with a growth target of 6 per cent per annum.[13] As far as incomes policy was concerned, the General Council still supported a voluntary policy and advised TUC affiliates to aim at a flat-rate increase of 14*s* per week per employee. Its attitude towards the government's statutory provisions was, however, becoming yet more hostile. The TUC Annual Conference voted against statutory incomes policy by a majority of 7:1, while

76

at the Labour Party Conference a motion moved by Cousins calling for the repeal of all incomes policy legislation was passed by a majority of 5:1. In fact the government continued to be lax in its enforcement of incomes policy in 1968 and 1969. Fewer and fewer cases were referred to the NBPI and a plethora of bogus productivity deals was allowed through. That the annual increase in hourly earnings was a mere 7.5 per cent in 1968 can be explained by the government's severely deflationary policies and the fact that in the aftermath of devaluation food and consumer prices as a whole rose less than other prices.[14]

IV
In Place of Strife

It is evident that from mid 1968 the government was increasingly frustrated and disillusioned by the operation of incomes policy and in particular its failure to restrain the inflation of pay over the previous three and a half years. These feelings were compounded by anguish at the susceptibility of British industry to unofficial strike action with its sudden and damaging effects on output. Over the next year Labour was to change the emphasis in its labour market policies from wage restraint to reform of industrial relations law. Wage drift, or the growth of earnings above and beyond nationally negotiated wage rates, had undermined Labour's incomes policy. Three main elements made up the difference between national wage rates and total earnings; all were extremely hard to monitor or control effectively. First, and most important, were piecework or bonus schemes of payment by result (PBB), which at this time were earned by nearly half of all workers in the manufacturing sector and which on their own accounted for an element in overall pay inflation equivalent to the underlying improvement in national productivity. As an NBPI report commented,

the essence of the problem of applying the incomes policy to PBR Systems is that a large part of the increase in earnings under them does not arise from 'claims' or 'settlements' in the accepted sense of the word, and they are often negotiated by individuals or small groups of workers with foremen, rate-fixers or first time management . . . Thousands of such bargains are struck every day . . . we came across only one instance where a firm was attempting to apply the [incomes] policy to PBR earnings in any way.[15]

Secondly, there were overtime earnings, and thirdly, plant rates paid in particular industries over and above the agreed company-wide rate.

The government, as the Donovan Commission on Trade Unions and

Employers' Associations recognized when its report was published in June 1968, was faced with the growth since the war of a two-tier bargaining system in the British labour market. The upper tier was the formal structure recognized by law, where bargaining took place between paid union officials and employers at industry level, and which the government was seeking to regulate. The second tier was informal, not subject to regulation by law, highly decentralized, and much more immediately sensitive to market forces. The Donovan Commission recommended that the shift from industry level to plant and company level bargaining should be recognized and encouraged, not least because it would help to link wages with productivity. Effective procedures should be developed voluntarily within the second tier to 'regulate actual pay, constitute a factory negotiating committee and grievance procedures which suit the circumstances, deal with such subjects as redundancy and discipline and cover the rights and obligations of Shop Stewards'. [16] Management was encouraged to take the lead.

The government was strongly influenced by Donovan and agreed with its basic analysis of Britain's industrial relations problem. However, rather than voluntaryism, the government initially favoured legislation to effect its recommendations. In January 1969 the Department of Employment and Productivity published the White Paper *In Place of Strife*,[17] which in addition to recommending a 'Commission of Industrial Relations' to encourage formalization of the informal sector, detailed legislation which would provide the government with legal authority to call a twenty-eight-day 'cooling-off period' when an unofficial strike was announced and to require a ballot before a strike could be classified 'official'. It was hoped these measures would help to tip the balance of power in collective bargaining more in favour of the employer. The unions were not at all impressed by the threat of permanent intervention of this kind into collective bargaining and made this clear during subsequent discussions with the government. In the summer, and despite Harold Wilson's strong support for the Bill, Cabinet agreed to drop the plans for legislation rather than face widespread industrial disruption and a possible major backbench revolt. Instead it accepted the TUC's 'solemn and binding' undertaking to implement a 'programme for action' of increased intervention in unconstitutional strikes and inter-union disputes.

By this time the government had to all intents and purposes allowed its formal incomes policy to lapse and had announced plans not to renew its extended powers over prices and incomes when they expired at the end of the year. The unions for their part were happy to take advantage of this. A final White Paper was, however, published in December 1969.[18] This document announced a rather unrealistic guiding light for pay increases of 2.5 per cent to 4.5 per cent. To guard against wage drift it suggested that where supplementary local bargains were struck in addition to those at national level, nationally negotiated wage settlements should include allowance for this. The level of settlement within the recommended range was also to bear relation to a variety of factors affecting the firm or industry: these being the rate of increase in labour productivity, the extent to which low-paid or women workers were involved and the labour market situation. It was further recommended that leeway be allowed for changes in the relative pay of different groups of workers. Exceptions to the guidelines were to depend on the same factors, and the twelve-month rule was to remain in operation. The White Paper also announced a plan to merge the NBPI with the Monopolies Commission to form a 'Commission for Industry and Manpower'. It was hoped that this body would help to tackle the problem of the fragmentation of wage-fixing by entrusting the task of defining pay for public servants and nationalized industry employees to a single body. The commission would also, on referral by a minister, examine the pay, prices, profits and dividends of firms above a certain size and pronounce whether or not a firm was acting contrary to the national interest in any of these spheres. Finally, the commission would investigate questions of industrial organization to see if structures should be so amended as to increase competition. A Bill to establish this commission was being debated when Parliament was dissolved in June 1970.

V
Wage Explosion 1969–70

During the final stages of Labour rule, pay and price inflation remained excessive, with the former gathering pace alarmingly, even though unemployment remained in excess of half a million throughout 1968 and 1969 and increased rapidly thereafter. Earnings were inflating at close to double figures in 1969, and in 1970 the figure grew to around 14 per cent. At the same time there was a marked increase in the number of days lost through strikes both official and unofficial, as Table 6.1 illustrates.

Table 6.1   *Industrial Relations in the 1960s*

	1960–61	1964–7	1968–71
No. of strikes	2,509	2,233	2,907
No. of strikers	576,000	655,000	1,264,000
No. of days lost (in thousands)	2,031	2,279	8,019

Source: K. Hawkins, *British Industrial Relations 1945–75* (London: Barrie & Jenkins, 1976), p. 136.

The pay and strike explosions of the years 1968–70 were very much interrelated and came as a disturbing surprise to those economists and politicians who put faith in an exact inverse relationship between unemployment and wage and price inflation. The reasons behind the explosion were multifarious and both economic and social in origin. Part of the cause was the unofficial breakdown of incomes policy and the efforts of workers to catch up on opportunities missed while it was more effectively in operation. The inflationary impetus of this process was exacerbated by the fact that public sector employees, whose total pay relied on a single tier of national agreements more than did that of their private sector counterparts, felt that despite the promises of Labour's 1964 manifesto, they had been particularly hard done by. They sought to re-establish rapidly their old relatives. One delegate from the National and Local Government Officers' Association (NALGO) told the TUC Annual Conference in 1968 that

there has not been a single White Paper, nor has there been a piece of prices and incomes legislation from either the present or the previous government, which has not contained discriminatory provisions against the public service.[19]

Furthermore, the low paid, whose income tended not to be affected so much by productivity agreements, also aggravated the rebound effect of the breakdown of incomes policy, as they sought to re-establish differentials operative before the productivity deal had become so popular and widespread. The effects of these two groups' discontent was further magnified by a general extension of comparability and the fact that relativities no longer always followed their traditional path. Taxation also played a role. From 1968 fiscal policy was pushing prices up and threatening real incomes. On the one hand the government's regular use of indirect taxation increased the prices of consumer goods, while on the other hand in the 1960s the typical manual worker found himself increasingly drawn into the direct taxation web. Until the later 1950s a manual worker had hardly been liable for income tax at all. By 1970–71 his tax and social insurance contributions took some 20 per cent of his earnings. The result of these taxation 'scissors' was a backlash from the taxpayer in the form of wage demands. Devaluation was a factor in the wage explosion too, but as we have seen, not one to overestimate.

These more immediate causes for the wage explosion of 1969–70 were compounded by some less obvious and more long-term explanations. In the first place, by the mid 1960s the increased wealth of the mass of the population had in itself led to a demand for greater continuity in income growth. The increasing numbers of capital goods being purchased, such as cars, washing machines and so on, demanded steadily expanding real incomes to meet payments. In the mid 1960s the rate of growth of real 'take home' pay had dropped to about 0.5 per cent per annum from 1.5 per cent in the early 1960s. People were not willing to accept this for long. Secondly, there is evidence, in the wake of more than twenty years of more or less steadily rising prices, of an enhanced inflation-consciousness which motivated negotiators to build in a contingency element into their wage claims. Added to these factors we must take account of the fact that full employment had been maintained without a break since the war and thus the fear of an imminent slump no longer served to temper wage claims at all. Lastly, there is evidence of a combined growing tide of militancy among shop stewards and some trade union leaders, as they came to realize more and more the power they possessed, particularly as technological advance enabled relatively small groups to exert a major impact on the economy through industrial action.

VI
Conclusions

What conclusions can we draw from Labour's employment and wage policies in the years 1964–70? The first point to make is that the Wilson government of the 1960s involved itself in the labour market more than any previous peacetime government, and the ultimate results can hardly be described as satisfactory. In the end, while Labour succeeded in leaving the incoming Conservative government a healthy balance of payments surplus, it also bequeathed a legacy of rising unemployment, a wage explosion and in increasingly militant and unpopular trade union movement acutely sensitive to the most minor infringement upon the process of free collective bargaining. There was, in short, little for which Edward Heath could be thankful.

Incomes policy was seen initially as a means to reform the collective bargaining process in this country by consent. It was a policy with a long-term goal which would hopefully prove conducive to prolonged economic expansion and growth. The failure of the government to tailor its demand-management polices more adequately and swiftly to suit more responsibility in the determination of pay, the unsuitability of the British trade union movement for its prescribed role in the incomes policy, and the development of certain unforeseen and unhelpful circumstances, meant that the emphasis in incomes policy had to revert increasingly over the years 1965 and 1966 to negative, out-and-out and legally backed restraint in an effort to maintain the external value of sterling. The hopes for reform of the collective bargaining system were undermined as much as anything by wage drift and payment by results systems in particular, in the context of a tightening labour market. One must conclude that Labour had come to power committed to an incomes policy without really having an adequate grasp of the mechanisms of the labour market. Furthermore, Alec Cairncross's criticism in 1961 of government departments' knowledge of these matters had obviously also largely fallen on deaf ears. Hence, the Wilson government was forced to learn on the job, by which time it was too late.

The policy of wage restraint of 1966–7 did seem to have some temporary success in curbing wage and price inflation in late 1966 and early 1967, but it was too inflexible and draconian to last long and in any case failed to prevent devaluation. In the aftermath of devaluation the government's major aim became making devaluation work. The watchwords of the later 1960s were austerity and stagnation as deflation rather than formal incomes policy became the major tool to turn the external account round. By mid 1968 the government had become increasingly frustrated and disillusioned with formal incomes policy and came to the conclusion that the best means to restrict the growth of incomes was by trying to tip the scales in favour of the employers in the collective bargaining process particularly on the shop floor. As such, the government shifted its target to what the Donovan Commission described as the second tier of industrial relations. It was, however, forced to drop its proposals in this respect because of political pressures, but one must question how successful the provisions of *In*

Place of Strife would have been in any case, given the strength of the forces pushing up wages in the late 1960s and the fact that the first tier of industrial relations was by this time largely being left to its own devices.

The changing nature of Labour's policies to control wage inflation meant that the NBPI, originally set up as a reformist, educative body, soon found itself in an ineffectual limbo, unsure exactly where it stood, or what its proper role was. Fewer and fewer cases were referred to it, and those on which it did pass judgement tended not to be the most important. Indeed, especially when incomes policy was tightened, the really vital wage claims as far as the economy was concerned were deliberately kept away from the NBPI to avoid confrontation. The seamen's claim of 1966 is a case in point. Alex Jarrat, the secretary of the NBPI, has described the board's difficulties as follows:

The fact that it was subject to sporadic and often unsuitable references made it very difficult to develop a sufficiently coherent 'case law' for incomes policy.[20]

In an effort to provide some much-needed flexibility and to hold incomes policy together after 1967, the NBPI took up the cause of productivity agreements. Unfortunately, these soon became a means to drive a horse and cart through the policy. In a retrospective survey of twenty-four productivity deals struck under Labour's incomes policies; Hugh Clegg found that over half were spurious or seriously defective.[21]

The use of price controls and guidelines was, despite all the government's talk of a *prices* and incomes policy, never something to which Labour attached a great deal of faith. They should be seen as much as anything as a necessary political counterweight to wages policy. The government had to be seen to be doing something about prices in order to secure trade union support for wage restraint. They were never easy to police and were frequently circumvented by the cross-subsidization of prices not specifically mentioned on the government's lists. Furthermore, throughout its term of office, Labour's indirect taxation policies were inconsistent with its announced plans to keep prices down as much as possible. The trade unions were certainly never convinced by the government's rhetoric about price control. Jarrat, who as much as anyone should have been in a position to gauge opinion, has written that

the policy failed almost completely to convince people that it was a prices and incomes policy.[22]

7

Mr Heath,
Incomes Policy and the
Miners 1970–74

I
'Selsdon Man', 'N-I' and the
Industrial Relations Act

While in opposition the Tories held a series of conferences for industrialists and academics to discuss certain policy issues and to formulate strategies for government. The most famous of these conferences was that held at Selsdon Park in January 1970 from which emerged the liberal philosophy that dominated Conservative economic policy in 1970 and 1971. The Tories emphasized the need for less, but more efficient, government and to create a beneficial and supportive environment for the private sector. The superiority of the market was to be restored and the frontiers of the state rolled back. As far as the wages problem was concerned, the Tories' election manifesto was quite clear; 'we utterly reject the philosophy of compulsory wage control', it stated. [1] Wage inflation would be curbed in the long term by reducing the power of the trade unions by law and thus creating a freer labour market. The Tories were in no way deterred by Labour's experiences with *In Place of Strife* and believed themselves to be supported by the mass of public opinion in wishing to clip the wings of the unions.

When Heath's government took over the reins of power, however, earnings were inflating at an annual rate of some 14 per cent and thus it felt compelled to do something about the wages problem in the short term. The government could not wait until its industrial relations legislation was operative. Its response was a dual-edged policy which it

84

saw as broadly consistent with its non-interventionist stance. On the one hand the Tories intended to hold unemployment at around half a million to dampen inflationary pressure. As such they were willing to rely partially on the Phillips Curve relationship, despite its recent failings. Secondly, they recognized the role the government played as a direct employer and decided to give a strong lead on wages in the public sector in the hope that private sector employers would follow their example. Each successive major settlement in the public sector was to be 1 per cent less than the last.

This policy became know as 'de-escalation', or the 'N-I strategy'. It was not overly successfully in its early stages. The electricity supply workers broke through it almost immediately and during most of 1971 pay settlements remained in double figures. It was only in the last quarter of that year that wage inflation fell to single figures, by which time price inflation had come down to 6 per cent and unemployment, in the wake of the monetary squeeze of 1969–70, had risen dramatically to 900,000, or some 4 per cent of the working population. Evidence also shows that public sector manual workers actually fared better than private sector manual workers in 1971 and 1972.[2] The 'N-I' policy was abandoned in early 1972 when the National Union of Mineworkers (NUM) challenged it successfully. The NUM wanted a 30 per cent wage increase to offset the slide in their relative earnings of the 1960s. The National Coal Board (NCB) initially offered only 8 per cent in line with the 'de-escalation' policy, and the result was a work-to-rule followed by an all-out strike. Because of the secondary picketing of power stations, coal stocks were rendered useless and the dispute led rapidly to power cuts and a three-day week. The ensuing industrial dislocation and public resentment forced the government to seek a compromise solution. A special court of inquiry recommended a settlement of 20 per cent and the miners obtained further concessions during direct negotiations with the Prime Minister.

Following the breakdown of the 'N-I' strategy, the government dramatically reorientated its economic policies. The philosophy of 'Selsdon Man' was quickly abandoned. Not only had 'de-escalation' been shattered and unemployment risen dramatically towards the politically sensitive 1 million mark, but its industrial relations legislation was already proving ineffective. The Industrial Relations Act had been passed in August 1971. Its major element was the prohibition of the 'closed shop' except where unions could prove that 100 per cent membership was essential to their survival in a particular place of work.

The 'closed shop' was viewed as the foundation of the trade union movement's monopoly power, without which its ability to negotiate excessive wage increases would be undermined, and its capacity to organize an effective strike reduced. The Industrial Relations Act also placed limitations on legal immunities from damages arising from strikes. The Act provided that only trade unions and their agents registered with the government and their agents could induce persons to break contracts in furtherance of a trade dispute. This provision sought to attack shop stewards' power by making them liable for damage arising from unofficial strike action and was an inducement for trade unions to register under the Act so that they could escape liability for strikes. Additionally, agreements between unions and employers were to be binding in law unless a clause was specifically inserted to the contrary. Unions thus had an obligation to make sure members obeyed collective agreements. If not they could be sued at a new Industrial Relations Court. Finally the Act contained provisions which empowered the Secretary of State for Employment to apply to the new court for a 'cooling-off' period of sixty days so that he could postpone any industrial action likely to prove injurious to the national economy, security, or public health and safety, and would allow him to check that a union's membership supported strike action by forcing it to conduct a ballot.

The TUC Annual Conference of September 1971 voted by a majority of 5.6 million votes to 4.5 million votes to instruct its members not to register under the new Act. Union reaction to the Act was in general extremely hostile, especially as it sought to attack the 'closed shop' for which the unions had fought for so long, and as the government had refused to consult with them at any stage prior to its coming into operation. They refused to co-operate and indeed launched a major campaign against the legislation. At the same time, employers, anxious not to stir up an already explosive situation, neglected to use the Act. As a result the legislation proved to be of very limited value.

II
'U'-Turn and Incomes Policy
Phase I

In the mean time the steady rise in unemployment was a major political embarrassment to the government. The Tories had never sought to allow it to rise to such a level and were faced with pressure from all sides to do something about it. In fact successive small reflationary packages had been introduced throughout 1971, including one assembled in response to an offer by the Confederation of British Industries (CBI) to ask its members to limit price increases to 5 per cent over the year to July 1972. However, despite a forecast of 3.5 per cent growth for 1972, these measures appeared to be having little effect on the employment figures in the early months of 1972, and a further major stimulus of some £1,200 million was injected into the economy in the budget in the hope of producing an annual growth rate of 5 per cent and bringing unemployment back down to 500,000. The Chancellor, Anthony Barber, also announced his willingness to free the exchange rate if necessary, in order to override any balance of payments constraint and keep expansion going.

The reorientation of macroeconomic policy demanded that the government take new action to check wage and price inflation. Edward Heath had never been overly keen on the economics of Selsdon Park and felt that he could sit down with both sides of industry and convince them of the need for restraint in the new expansionary environment. He seems to have been impressed by the success his friend Willy Brandt had had in talking to the unions in Germany and thought he could achieve similar results in the United Kingdom. His task, however, was never going to be easy. The institutional background to industrial relations in Britain is far more complicated than is the case in Germany and the unions' attitude towards the government was at that time soured by the furore over the Industrial Relations Act, ministers' *laissez-faire* rhetoric of much of the last two years and the rising tide of unemployment. Moreover, real post-tax income had grown on average by some 4 per cent per annum in the years 1970–72. The trade unions would not easily be convinced of the need to end free collective bargaining, especially at a time when the leadership of two of the largest unions, the Amalgamated Union of Engineering Workers (AUEW) and the NUM, had shifted to the left. But this is not to deny that there were some fragile foundations which could be built on. For example, as early as the 1970 TUC Annual Conference, the General Secretary, Victor Feather, had suggested that the two sides of industry got together with the government to thrash out a viable expansionist policy, and in August 1971 an NEDC sub-committee had discussed the 'threshold payments' favoured by both the CBI and TUC as a means to reduce wage claims and dampen down inflation.

Introductory and informal discussions between government,

employers and unions were held in the spring of 1972, but these achieved little of substance. By the summer, however, the government became increasingly anxious to get some kind of agreement on wages, not least because it had by this time set sterling free and was worried it might plummet if speculators thought inflation was likely to run out of control. Eventually in July both the CBI and TUC agreed to more formal discussions on the economic situation within the context of the NEDC. The CBI consented to extend its price control initiative for an extra three months to provide a positive environment and the government proposed to hold the meetings at 10 Downing Street and Chequers to underline their importance.

The meetings to thrash out a viable voluntary prices and incomes policy continued until early November. The TUC was represented by its usual NEDC personnel of Jack Jones (TGWU), Hugh Scanlon (AUEW), Vic Feather, Lord Cooper, Lord Allen and Lord Green, the government by Heath, Barber and the Employment Secretary, Maurice Macmillan, plus Sir Douglas Allen, the Permanent Secretary to the Treasury, and another senior Treasury official, Sir William Armstrong. The CBI delegation was headed by its director general, Campbell Adamson, but by all accounts the CBI did not really play a large part in the talks.

At first the government did not seek to push a general norm for wage increases. Instead it concentrated on other wage-related issues. The unions for their part sought to extend the discussion to the Industrial Relations Act and the general management of the economy. Progress was distinctly slow, with various sub-committees examining the issues of low pay and how to curb rising prices. In the mean time the TUC Annual Conference passed a resolution with a rather familiar ring to it. It stated that

no consideration can be given to any policy on incomes unless it is an integral part of an economic strategy which includes control of rents, profits, dividends and prices, and is designed to secure a redistribution of income and wealth nationally and globally.[3]

It was not until 26 September that the government first put forward a real initiative for wage restraint. It proposed that there should be a voluntary wage increase limitation of £2 per worker per week. Taking into account wage drift this was expected to yield an average increase of £2.60 or around 8 per cent on average earnings. Overall price increases were to be limited voluntarily to 5 per cent wherever possible. Threshold payments of 20 pence for each 1 per cent increase in the retail price index beyond 6 per cent could be negotiated. The government would extend its growth target of 5 per cent to the next two years and pensions would be increased in line with national prosperity. Furthermore, Heath offered both the TUC and the CBI what he called a 'real partnership' in the management of the economy, involving regular meetings to review policy.

The General Council's response to these proposals was to reject them. But rather than risk deflation and/or a statutory policy by pulling out of discussions completely, it tabled a series of detailed counter-proposals. Since 1966 the TUC had been undertaking serious and detailed investigations into planning and economic policy. It was as keen as any group to improve Britain's economic performance, and in each annual *Economic Review* it had presented its own analysis of the economic situation and a series of measures it saw as relevant to Britain's problems at that time. The proposals it expounded to the government in 1972 were very much the result of these investigations. In the middle of October it suggested that the government commit itself to 6 per cent growth. It also made it clear that it believed the government had underestimated the share of national income taken up by wages and salaries and therefore their prospective share of any increase in national income. Moreover, it believed the government had overestimated the total number of employees and had thus tabled too modest a wage norm. It wanted an average weekly wage increase of £3.40, although it warned that by disturbing established wage structures, a flate-rate, across-the-board norm might well store up problems for later. On threshold payments, it wanted 30 pence for each 1 per cent rise above 5 per cent in the retail price index. As far as prices were concerned, it put the case for comprehensive and statutory control, the introduction of value added tax (VAT) at a lower rate than the government was proposing, renegotiation of the EEC's Common Agricultural Policy, and the freezing of public housing rents. It also sought increases in pensions and family allowances, the shift limitation of dividends, the introduction of a wealth tax, and last but not least, the non-operation of the Industrial Relations Act.

When the TUC's demands were discussed at the NEDC some progress was made on the issue of the flat-rate basic wage increase, but the price control proposals created more problems. The CBI felt that it could not accept statutory price control in the absence of statutory wage control. Heath was also understandably worried that he would have difficulty obtaining agreement to the policy from within his own party. On 30 October he told the TUC that it would have to decide between an all-statutory or an all-voluntary agreement. The TUC found itself in a difficult position. Its representatives were now certain that the government would introduce statutory wage controls if no agreement was reached soon. What is more they would likely be represented as the villains of the piece in the event of any breakdown. They were split as to whether or not they should break off the talks, until Vic Feather convinced the General Council it should agree to a compromise proposition whereby the government would guarantee and act to ensure that food prices would rise no faster than 5 per cent during the period of pay restraint.

At the next tripartite meeting the Prime Minister replied to this new initiative by saying that the TUC had still not faced up to the essential issue of statutory or voluntary control, while adding that it would be extremely difficult to guarantee retail prices. The following day the Prime Minister opened up what was to be the last in this series of discussions by reiterating the government's position of 26 September, while adding that the proposal for a 5 per cent voluntary prices ceiling should not apply to prices heavily influenced by import cost increases, and offering some minor concessions with regard to rents, rates, welfare payments and pensions. Moreover, he emphasized that there were certain areas of policy which had to remain the domain of government and Parliament alone and which would not be subject to discussion in any tripartite forum. He was, of course, referring to the Industrial Relations Act above all. The TUC delegation's unanimous conclusion was that since the government appeared to have gone back on its promise of a 'real partnership' in the management of the economy, there was no longer any basis for discussion. Furthermore, with the exclusion of import prices and with them many foodstuffs from the government's 'price guarantee', the package offered was now much less attractive. Four days later the government introduced a statutory pay policy, and in the words of one senior official, over the remainder of the Tories' period of office, 'life in the Treasury was dominated by the attempt to make this policy work'.[4]

It has been suggested in the light of the government's 'take it or leave it' ultimatum of the final meeting that it really never wanted to reach agreement at all and merely saw the tripartite discussions as a means to drum up public support for a statutory policy. This seems rather implausible and a closer examination of the facts reveals that the government had extremely good reason to seek a swift conclusion to the discussions in November. In the first place the CBI's price initiative had expired at the end of October. Secondly, from July pay settlements had shown a dramatic upward shift from an average of some 11 per cent to around 17 per cent in anticipation of an incomes policy announcement. The establishment of a new and higher going rate would make it all the more difficult to get a voluntary policy to hold in the 1972–3 wage round. Furthermore, the exact details of the freeze itself were only put together over the weekend following the break-down of discussions.[5] Had the government always intended to bring in a statutory policy, one would have expected it to have made better contingency plans.

Some doubts have also been cast over the trade unions' attitude in these discussions. They certainly did not want to hand the government a political victory on a plate and their leaders were also doubtful about being able to make a voluntary policy stick with the rank and file. Moreover, some union leaders, including Clive Jenkins of the white collar workers' union, the Association of Scientific, Technical and Managerial Staffs (ASTMS), and Ray Buckton of the train drivers' union, the Associated Society of Locomotive Engineers and Firemen (ASLEF), announced that in any event they would not bind their members to an agreement with the Tories. It does seem, however, that despite some reservations, the TUC did want to reach an agreement if it was possible. It had good reason to fear the alter-natives, while some of the more moderate trade unionists were anxious to establish a degree of order in collective bargaining, which to their mind was becoming increasingly chaotic.

The reasons behind the failure to reach agreement were more complex than a mere disinclination to do so. Suspicion of the other side's motives certainly came into the equation. How could it be otherwise given the state of government–union relations over the preceding years? But the most important reason seems to have lain in the differing philosophies of the two sides. The TUC saw the talks as a major extension of collective bargaining, while the government, for all its rhetoric about a 'real partnership' in the running of the economy, was more worried about finding a particular method to solve a particular problem. As Edward Heath said later, 'these talks weren't carried out as a bargaining session', but rather as an effort 'to find a rational way of handling ... economic problems and to try and get people to agree on the figures'.[6] The government was only ever willing to offer limited concessions, and these had to be restricted in the main to macroeconomic matters and be in keeping with what it saw as the scope provided by its stabilization policy.

In short the TUC had to accept something fairly close to the goverment's final offer for success. This was insufficient for the TUC General Council to be able to believe it could gain the support of the rank and file. The key element was the government's unwillingness to offer anything like a cast-iron guarantee on prices.

The details of the Tories' statutory wage freeze were published in a White Paper entitled *A Programme for Controlling Inflation: the First Stage*, released on 6 November.[7] All rates of remuneration were to be held constant for a period of ninety days, while the only price increases admissible were to be those pertaining to fresh foods, or where material prices rose particularly sharply. The policy closely followed that in operation in the United States at the time and was accompanied by action to control the rate of growth of the money supply, which at that stage, if one takes sterling M3 as the best indicator, was running at close to 30 per cent per annum.[8] The wage freeze held despite the TUC's verbal protests and between November 1972 and March 1973 average earnings rose by less than 1 per cent. The retail price index scarcely moved either. The TUC failed to mount any concerted campaign to challenge the freeze. Its opposition was limited because several of the most important groups had already obtained large settlements before the freeze, the freeze was in any case going to be short-lived, and there was a general reluctance to defy the law.

III

Incomes Policy Phase II

Early in 1973, after a further series of brief and unprofitable meetings with the TUC, the government set out in a series of White Papers the second stage of its counter-inflation strategy, which again borrowed heavily from the US model.[9] This was to last from April to October of that year. The policy on pay and prices was to be monitored by a new Pay Board and a new Price Commission. In contrast to the NBPI, which could merely review cases referred to it by government, and could only impose limited delays on wage and price increases, the two new bodies were to have real power to control wages and prices. All firms employing more than 100 workers had to provide them with wage, price and profit information, and prior approval from the Pay

Board was required for settlements affecting more than 1,000 workers. The two new bodies could order reductions in pay and price levels if they saw fit and punish evasion by heavy fines. The Pay Board was also given the job of producing two reports, one by mid September on the treatment of anomalies and the other by the end of 1973 on pay relativities.

The pay norm proposed by the government for this period was to be £1 plus 4 per cent of existing earnings. To temper wage drift the limit was to apply to the total increase in the wage bill of a bargaining unit and could be divided up among workers as negotiators saw fit. This was the equivalent of an 8 per cent increase, or half the going rate before the freeze. The only exceptions were for the realization of equal pay, and there was an absolute ceiling on wage and salary increases of £250 per annum. Price increases were to be limited to what was needed to cover increased production costs, and profits to the average of the best two years of the previous five. In addition, the government increased financial assistance to low-income rent payers faced with local authority rent increases, outlined its intention to increase old age pensions from October and to eliminate VAT from children's clothing, and renewed its commitment to a 5 per cent growth rate.

The General Council reacted harshly to the new policy and declined to nominate trade unionists for positions on the two new policing bodies. However, industrial resistance was still limited. The number of days lost through strike action in 1972 was lower than in the previous three years. As far as the result of stage II of the policy were concerned, the Pay Board claimed that the average pay increase resulting from approved stage II settlements was close to 8 per cent. However, during the seven months of stage II, earnings actually rose at an annual rate of some 15 per cent. Part of the reason lay in settlements postponed by the freeze, but the main explanation was the tightening of the labour market caused by the government's expansionary policies, which led piecework payments, bonuses and overtime rates to rise rapidly and caused highly competitive bidding between firms as unemployment fell rapidly towards 500,000. The budget of 1973 was neutral and left the PSBR at the high level of £4.4 billion in an effort to stimulate an investment boom, and despite the measures of the previous December, monetary growth (M3) remained in excess of 25 per cent per annum. These internal inflationary pressures were exacerbated by a world commodity price boom which saw non-oil commodity prices rise by 62 per cent in dollar terms in 1973, and by a 9 per cent devaluation of sterling between the fourth quarters of 1972 and 1973. Incomes policy was being asked to do far too much in an environment in no way conducive to its successful operation.

By the early summer of 1973 a new round of stock-building was under way, and the consensus of opinion within Whitehall was that the government should move towards restriction. May saw the announcement of cuts in public expenditure of £100 million in 1973–4 and £500 million in 1974–5, together with a plan to save a further £100 million or so in 1973–4 by rephasing building contracts. In July efforts were made to tighten monetary policy further. However, these measures cannot be described as a traditional 'stop', they were merely a slight deceleration. Brendan Sewill, the Chancellor's special assistant at this time, describes Treasury opinion like this:

The general view was ... that it would be wrong to slam on the brakes. With the hope that the rise in world prices might prove temporary, with the advantage of the decision in 1972 to allow the pound to float, with the success (at that time) of the counter inflation policy, both the Treasury and many experts outside felt – until the autumn of 1973 – that there was a reasonable chance that we might win through without another stop. [10]

As a result macroeconomic policy remained highly expansionary over the summer of 1973 and it was not until November 1973, in the midst of the oil crisis, that major deflationary action was taken in the form of £1,200 million of public expenditure cuts.

IV
Incomes Policy Phase III and the Miners

It was with this background, and in the knowledge that the rapid rise in food prices was turning public opinion against incomes policy, that the government began to think about a third stage of its counter-inflation policy. Both the CBI and the TUC were again invited to come and discuss the matter with it at an early stage. The latter agreed only reluctantly, and then only on receiving assurances that no topic would be excluded from discussions. After some highly unsatisfactory meetings the government eventually published its proposals for the year to November 1974 in early October in a Green Paper. The TUC had by this time reached agreement with the Labour Party on what was later to become the 'Social Contract', and made clear its disapproval of another round of statutory wage control. It failed, however, to offer any specific alterations. Thus the new code became operative for pay, profits, dividends and prices over the first week of November. Increases of up to 7 per cent per 'group' were to be allowed, or if it was preferred, £2.25 per head per week, with a maximum annual increase of £350 per year. A further 1 per cent would be made available for settlements which reduced anomalies and obstacles to the better use of manpower, and extra payments would also be allowed for proven increased efficiency or where price stability was encouraged, for unsocial hours and for progress towards equal pay. The package also included allowance for the negotiation of threshold payments. The aim was to take expectations out of wage bargaining. This was a radical departure for British incomes policy, which had always previously sought to weaken any link between pay and prices. Extra payments of 40 pence per week would be allowed for every 1 per cent rise in the retail price index above 7 per cent. The hope was to keep the growth in earnings to around 11 per cent over the next year. The price provisions under stage III remained very much as under stage II, although there was some slight relaxation.

The major assumption behind stage III was that inflation could be held to 7 per cent over the next year. This was optimistic, to say the least, given that inflation at that time had risen to 9.2 per cent, the movements of non-oil commodity prices and sterling, and the fact that the oil crisis had broken in the wake of the Middle East War. The policy had also been designed to allow a particularly large increase to the miners, who at the NUM Conference in July had adopted wage targets ranging from £8–£13 on basic rates, or some 22–46 per cent, and were making particularly militant noises at that time.

The government soon found itself faced by several groups threatening industrial action against stage III, but it was the miners' wage claim which was the real worry. When negotiations started between the NCB and the NUM, the employers made an offer of some 16.5 per cent, which maximized the use of the provisions for flexibility within the stage III guidelines and was stated to be 'final'. The miners, stiffened by the fact that the oil crisis had made coal a much more precious commodity, rejected the offer, and started an overtime ban on 12 November. The Pay Board could only interpret the policy as it stood and the government refused to allow the NCB to raise its offer. In the new year, by which time the government had introduced a three-day week to conserve energy supplies, several efforts were made to break the impasse. The TUC suggested that other unions should agree that special circumstances existed in the case of the miners, and so if a particularly large settlement was forthcoming, they would not use it as a yardstick for their own negotiations. The government was unconvinced, not least because the TUC did not in any case officially support the incomes policy. Towards the end of January the Pay Board's report on relativities was finally published and the Prime Minister invited the CBI and TUC to talks to set up an independent pay relativities body to consider major claims, including the miners'. However, on the same day the NUM held a ballot which showed 81 per cent of the membership in favour of a strike from 10 February. On 7 February the Prime Minister announced a general election would take place on 28 February. He sought by this to obtain a mandate to continue to fight the miners. The NUM rejected an invitation to postpone the strike until after the election even though its existing pay agreement was due to last until 1 March. During the strike and the election campaign the Pay Board sat to consider the miners' relative pay. Its report, published after the election, concluded that the miners did indeed have a considerable case. By this time, however, the election result had been declared, and Harold Wilson as head of a minority Labour government had succeeded Heath as Prime Minister. The worst nightmare of many of the officials in the Ministry of Labour in the immediate postwar era had come true. They had, of course, greatly feared statutory government intervention in wage determination because of its potential destabilizing effects on the political and democratic process.

V
Conclusions

Even allowing for the extremely difficult external circumstances of the years 1972–4, one cannot but conclude that Edward Heath's government got itself into the most awful mess and was responsible for a period of gross economic mismanagement. From 1972 its strategy of a combination of rapid expansion, depreciation of the exchange rate, and statutory incomes policy was fundamentally flawed. The pace of reflation was too great (Britain had never experienced a growth rate of 5 per cent per annum over a protracted period), the budget deficit allowed to expand too rapidly and monetary policy far too lax. The PSBR grew from a small negative figure in 1970 to some £6,300 million in 1974, while the excessive growth in the money supply is illustrated by Table 7.1.

Table 7.1 *Annual Rate of Growth in Sterling M3 1971–74 (per cent seasonally adjusted)*

1971	1	12.8	1973	1	25.4
	2	11.0		2	22.5
	3	10.9		3	27.0
	4	14.3		4	27.0
1972	1	18.5	1974	1	23.6
	2	24.9		2	18.6
	3	26.0		3	12.2
	4	26.8		4	10.1

Source: Central Statistical Office, *Economic Trends* (London: HMSO).

In this context incomes policy was always going to be working against the tide of a rapidly tightening labour market and, even if the provisions of the Industrial Relations Act had been adhered to, likely to prove prone to excessive wage drift. It was established in 1975 that there were some 5,700 pay settlements in the private sector which covered between 100 and 999 employees each. It was impossible for the government to ensure that all these settlements fell within its guidelines, and what of the settlements that covered less than 100 employees?[11] With the addition of a downward float of sterling there was little hope of protracted success, especially in the context of a worldwide commodity price boom, the fourfold rise in oil prices towards the end of 1973 and the continued operation of many of the factors which had helped to produce the wage explosion of the late 1960s. Table 7.2 shows the escalation in imported inflation in sterling terms from the time that the currency was set free to the time that Wilson's minority government came into office.

Table 7.2 *Imported Inflation in Sterling Terms (per cent per annum)*

1972	July to December	16
1973	January to June	28
	July to December	42
1974	January to June	64

Britain's relatively high propensity to import in comparison to countries such as the USA and Japan meant that these figures would have a large impact on retail prices and hence wages.

Heath involved his government in the workings of the labour market even more than the Wilson administration of the 1960s and in doing so left two legacies. First of all, his policies, and the system of threshold payments in particular, helped to further increase the inflation-consciousness of the workforce to the point where its sensitivity to price rises was such as to render any policy which depended for its success solely on an acquiescence postulate, such as originally suggested by Keynes, or on 'money-illusion', unlikely to succeed for anything but the shortest period. During the years 1959–64 nominal demand as measured by Money GDP grew by nearly 38 per cent; slightly over half of the growth was reflected in increased output and the rest in higher prices. The expansion in nominal demand was increased in subsequent periods, but more and more of it was reflected in inflation and less and less in higher output. Over the period 1974–9 the rise in nominal demand of nearly 130 per cent was reflected almost entirely in higher prices. [12]

The second legacy left by Heath's administration was an extreme antipathy amongst a large section of the Conservative Party towards any degree of monetary laxity, interventionist economic policies and formal incomes restraint in particular. They had no wish to see for a second time a Conservative government in the ignominious position in which Heath's administration found itself in early 1974. Thus the policies pursued between 1972 and 1974 and their failure go a long way towards explaining the triumph of Thatcherite economic liberalism within the Conservative Party. As such, many would argue that Heath has a lot to answer for.

8
Labour and the Social Contract 1974–9*

I
The Social Contract Part I: 1974–5

The five years of Labour rule between 1974 and 1979, like the last two years of Edward Heath's administration, were dominated by the politics of incomes restraint and efforts to make the various manifestations of their wages policy, or the 'Social Contract' as it became known, a success. The idea of a 'social contract' was first introduced by Thomas (Lord) Balogh soon after Labour's defeat in the 1970 election. Labour's failure to control union wage demands in the 1960s had, asserted Balogh, led to inflation and the need to introduce unpopular deflationary policies. When next in office Labour would need a workable long-term incomes policy, and to secure it in return would have to offer more socialist policies than before. Sacrifices in wage bargaining would only be forthcoming if the economy was planned systematically, welfare provisions were expanded, public ownership was extended and more progressive taxation introduced.[1] Balogh's notion of a 'social contract' was far removed from that embodied in the 1944 White Paper.

The virtues of rather less radical voluntary incomes policies were soon also being extolled by several prominent figures in the Labour Party, including Barbara Castle, Jim Callaghan and Tony Crosland,[2] but the trade unions, still embittered by their experiences of the 1960s, were not keen to discuss the subject. Hugh Scanlon and Jack Jones were particularly firm on this topic. Thus the Labour leadership came to spend a lot of time over the years 1970–72 trying to re-establish a

---

*Much of this chapter is drawn from W. H. Fishbein, *Wage Restraint by Consensus: Britain's Search for an Incomes Policy Agreement* 1965–79 (London: Routledge and Kegan Paul, 1984) chs 5–9.

trustworthy and workable relationship with the unions and to develop a credible policy for controlling inflation. The strategy which finally emerged in February 1973 in a joint Labour Party and TUC Statement on *Economic Policy and the Cost of Living* was to form the basis of the 'Social Contract'. It reflected a leftward shift in the balance of power within the Labour Party and encompassed much which had appeared in the TUC's *Economic Reviews*. It proposed 'direct action on the prices of those items which loom largest in budgets of workpeople, such as food, housing and rent', including 'a wide ranging and permanent system of price controls', together with subsidies, a new approach to housing policy and a large-scale redistribution of income and wealth. These measures, it was advanced, would yield a climate of responsible free collective bargaining and, coupled with a dirigiste and expansionary macroeconomic policy which would reduce the growth of unit labour costs, ease inflation. No mention was made of a more formal incomes policy than this and official Labour Party policy followed this line until the run-up to the election of February 1974.

Many senior Labour politicians blanched at what they saw as a glaring omission from their economic policies, but their efforts to make the TUC relent on this matter came to little. Labour's election manifesto of February 1974 could offer no more than the hope that a Labour government could draw upon trade union support in the fight against inflation:

We believe that the action we propose on prices together with an understanding with the TUC on the lines which we have already agreed, will create the right economic climate for money incomes to grow in line with production.[3]

Indeed, during the election campaign Harold Wilson felt compelled to give the impression that Labour had actually already secured a firm agreement from the unions on voluntary incomes policy, but after trade union denials, he was forced by the press to admit that this was not really the case.

In spite of this, however, the electorate, disillusioned with Heath's economic and industrial relations mismanagement, voted the Labour Party into the largest number of seats, and Wilson was once again installed as Prime Minister, this time at the head of a minority government. Armed with a seemingly flawed economic policy, he was faced with Britain's most serious economic crisis since the war. In addition to dealing with the industrial dislocation caused by the coal strike and the three-day week, he saw the rate of inflation jump 5 percentage points to nearly 16 per cent over the first six months of

1974. Earnings were easily outstripping prices throughout this period, while the trends in economic growth and unemployment had reversed alarmingly. Moreover, the current balance was showing an all-time record deficit.

The new government's first priority was to end the coal strike. The NCB was given permission to negotiate without regard to incomes policy limitations and two days after Labour came to power the NUM accepted a rise of approximately 30 per cent: about the same size of settlement as recommended by the Pay Board on the basis of their relativities procedure.

In his first budget, rather than cutting expenditure to take account of the massive oil price increase of 1973, Chancellor Denis Healey decided to maintain current expenditure plans, and to fulfil the government's promises to the trade unions and borrow to meet the deficit. Although the budget of March 1974 raised income tax, it included additional spending of £1,240 million in a full twelve months on pensions and other benefits, a further £500 million for food subsidies and £350 million for housing. In a further financial statement in July, VAT and rates were reduced in anticipation of an autumn election. In 1982 Joel Barnett, then Chief Secretary to the Treasury and Healey's 'number two' at the Treasury, summed up his feelings about this electioneering:

it might be said that the first months of the new Government were characterized by our spending money which in the event we did not have ... we should have been increasing indirect taxes, not reducing them.[4]

The government's saving grace was that it acted to engineer a rapid deceleration in monetary growth.

It was also not long before Wilson and Healey began to try to obtain a firmer agreement on wages policy. The ageing left-wing radical Michael Foot was appointed as Employment Secretary in an effort to talk the unions round and the TUC was persuaded to offer its support for the government's decision to retain stage III of the Tories' incomes policy until its legislative mandate expired in July. But this was only in an effort to ensure an orderly return to free collective bargaining and to head off the opposition's threat to bring down the government unless this was done or a viable substitute policy introduced. Unfortunately the decision to retain stage III implied continued provision for threshold payments. There were 14 million people whose wages included some form of indexation and all in all the threshold was to be triggered eleven times as price inflation proceeded at a higher rate than was forecast in the autumn of 1973. This greatly accelerated the wage–price spiral.

In June 1974 the General Council unanimously approved a document entitled *Collective Bargaining and the Social Contract* detailing TUC policy for the 1974–5 wage round (this contained the first official use of the term 'Social Contract').[5] The General Council advised negotiators to seek settlements 'claiming compensation for the rise in the cost of living since the last settlement'; bearing in mind that threshold payments would already have offered some compensation for price inflation. Alternatively, negotiators could seek to secure wage levels designed to match the rate of inflation over the next round. To further ensure a smooth transition from statutory control to free collective bargaining, the twelve-month rule between wage increases was to be retained. Finally, it was recommended that priority be given to agreements which would reduce unit costs (that is, productivity agreements), encourage 'reasonable minimum standards of pay' and equal pay, or improve non-wage benefits.

The General Council was in effect asking negotiators to seek to maintain the real income of their members. The problem was that the deterioration in Britain's balance of payments at that time required a movement of resources into exports and away from imports and consumption approximately equivalent to a 5 per cent decline in real incomes. Furthermore, the various loopholes and exceptions to the general rule would allow wage increases above the cost of living, especially when no system of vetting of wage claims or sanctions against recalcitrant unions existed. It was highly unlikely, therefore, that even a stabilization in living standards could be achieved, especially when neither government nor unions sought to go out of their way to publicize the policy. In the spring and summer of 1974 a series of individual union conferences passed a number of resolutions calling for very large wage increases. The going rate was soon established for 1974–5 at around 30 per cent. This militant behaviour owed much to the fact that public sector employees had again suffered a relative decline in wages, this time as a result of the Conservatives' incomes policy. In addition, the triumph of the miners added weight to the notion that unions, particularly those in strategically placed industries and occupations, could do very well for themselves by using aggressive negotiating tactics. The most important factor, however, was fear: fear of what was going to happen to the cost of living. The effect of the oil crisis on prices, added to the psychological effect of threshold payments on people's perceptions of the inflationary outlook and the continued operation of some of the factors we have already identified as affecting wage bargaining in the later 1960s, came together to produce a desperate struggle to keep earnings up with, and ahead of, inflation.

Labour's manifesto for the October 1974 election described the 'Social Contract' as being 'at the heart . . . of our programme to save the nation'.[6] When however they had been returned to power with an overall majority of three, wage demands of an unprecedented size, often coupled with the threat of industrial action, continued to be advanced in all sectors of the economy. Furthermore the number of days lost in strike action in the last quarter of 1974 was around twice as many as in the corresponding period in the previous year, and higher than any period since 1969. The General Council issued a circular reminding affiliates of the 'Social Contract' provisions, but this had no effect. Few settlements fell below 20 per cent in the period July to December 1974 and some reached as high as 40 per cent. The average growth in basic wages approached 27 per cent, while price inflation was a mere 17 per cent. Real incomes were being much more than maintained.

The realization that the 'Social Contract' was proving a disaster led to a succession of appeals from outsiders for the government to tighten up the policy. Even TUC General Secretary Len Murray suggested that the General Council amend its wage guidelines to stop wage increases anticipating future inflation, and reduce the number of 'special case' awards. This was rejected by other union leaders as it was deemed unfair to change the rules of collective bargaining in the middle of a wage round. During the remainder of the 1974–5 wage round, the miners, electricity supply workers, engineering workers and railwaymen all obtained huge increases. Wages and earnings were rising at an annual rate of more than 30 per cent, with prices not far behind. This inflation dwarfed the rates in most other industrialized nations and was a major factor behind the large payments deficits of 1974 and 1975. Fears were widespread of hyperinflation, and there was even talk of a threat to democracy. Had it not been for an influx of petrodollars and substantial borrowing the pound would have dived. The rate of wage inflation, the retention of price controls for most of 1974 and the tight monetary conditions also led to a major liquidity crisis and a collapse in industrial production and investment.

Table 8.1   *UK Monetary Conditions 1974–5*

		Sterling M3 (percentage growth per annum seasonally adjusted)	Prices (percentage growth per annum)
1974	1	23.6	12.7
	2	18.6	15.8
	3	12.2	16.9
	4	10.1	18.1
1975	1	7.9	20.3
	2	8.4	24.3
	3	10.4	26.6
	4	6.0	25.3

Source: Central Statistical Office, *Economic Trends* (London: HMSO).

By April 1975 unemployment had reached 850,000 (3.5 per cent) and was rising. The last time it had touched such a level (mid 1971) the government had reflated. Healey, by contrast, deflated, raising both direct and indirect taxation and cutting public expenditure by £1,100 million. Thus the budget of 1975 marks a major benchmark in postwar economic history. It signalled the suspension of the commitment to full employment as it had been known since 1945.

The blame for the failure of the 'Social Contract' during the 1974–5 wage round can in no way be put on the government. It fulfilled its side of the bargain in most respects. Its only real failing was in respect to full employment. As far as social expenditure and labour market legislation to strengthen the position of trade unionists were concerned it had done much as the trade unions desired. It was the unions who failed to deliver. As Joel Barnett put it,

the only give and take in the Contract was that the Government gave and the unions took. We did not give in to all their demands for more and more public expenditure in every field from child benefits to pensions, from industrial support to special employment measures, but we did more than we could afford.[7]

Sir Leo Pliatzky, a senior Treasury official at this time, reflecting on the growth in real terms in public expenditure of 12.2 per cent in Labour's first year in office, called it 'in some ways a period of collective madness'.[8] We have already examined the reasons behind the tide of union militancy in 1974–5, but why did the unions' leaders not exert a greater restraining influence over their members at this time in line with their promises to the government? The major reason lay in the fact that the shop stewards were ruling the roost at this stage. Contrary to what the Donovan Commission had predicted, the voluntary reform of the collective bargaining process did not lead to national trade union headquarters exercising greater control over wage determination. The number of full-time union officials was never raised sufficiently to handle the enormous increase in the number of negotiations effected by the movement from industry level to plant level bargaining. The fate of the 'Social Contract' depended on the mood of the rank and file and the shop stewards, not the national leaders, and in the uncertain economic environment of 1974–5 they were not interested in restraint.

II
The Social Contract Part II: 1975–6

According to one of Harold Wilson's closest aides, the Prime Minister saw it as impossible for him to remain as head of a government which went back on its word not to introduce a statutory incomes policy.[9] Furthermore, several senior Cabinet colleagues, including Michael Foot, were also ready to resign rather than see such a policy introduced. Perhaps only Roy Jenkins and Reg Prentice, both soon to defect from Labour's ranks, were ready wholeheartedly to back such a policy. However, a pseudo-statutory incomes policy was put to Cabinet towards the end of 1974, when Prices and Consumer Affairs Minister Shirley Williams tabled a proposal to prevent firms from passing large wage increases on to prices by using statutory price controls. This was dropped in the face of CBI and TUC opposition. The former thought it would exacerbate the profits squeeze, the latter saw it as little different from direct statutory wage restraint.

After the budget of 1975, however, the unions began to realize that the wages 'free for all' was not in the best long-term interest of the country or themselves, especially when the Chancellor warned them of more unpalatable deflationary medicine if they did not offer to do something about wage inflation before the end of July. They were also keen to keep Labour in office at a time when its parliamentary survival was increasingly threatened by opposition criticism of its economic policies. In late May Jack Jones, once the most outspoken critic of incomes policy, made a public plea for the universal application of a single flat-rate wage increase over the next wage round which would be worked out with the CBI. By early June, the TUC's research staff were preparing a policy paper which emphasized the need to get inflation below 20 per cent in the near future. Both the TUC Economic Committee and the General Council soon came to support an approach to the government and the CBI based on the following proposals: the setting of a price target for mid 1976, the announcement of a universal flat-rate pay increase bearing this in mind, the freezing of the incomes of the well paid, radical action to restrict price increases including the exclusion of subsidies, and the announcement of measures to reduce unemployment.

Tripartite discussions were held in late June, at which point confidence in sterling finally began to collapse. There have been rumours since that the Treasury, having little faith in voluntary restraint, precipitated this crisis in order to force the government into grasping the nettle of a statutory pay policy.[10] Nicholas Kaldor, the government's Chief Economic Adviser, has denied this, as indeed has Sir Leo Pliatzky. While the Treasury was sceptical about the type of restraint offered by the unions, it was also, 'after the trauma of the closing days of the Heath Government . . . highly conscious of the problems of enforcing a statutory policy'.[11] Whatever the immediate cause of the run on sterling, on 1 July Denis Healey issued an ultimatum to the unions. Inflation had to be brought down to single figures by the end of 1976: they could either accept an effective and workable voluntary incomes policy to facilitate this, or face a statutory policy enforced by sanctions on employers. Healey was in fact playing a dangerous game of political 'Russian roulette'. Had the unions called his bluff several Cabinet members would probably have resigned; in any case, it was doubtful whether he would have got a statutory policy through Parliament.

The following day in a meeting with the Economic Committee Healey, Foot and Williams took a hard line in pushing for a flat-rate across-the-board increase of £6 a week and maintaining that comprehensive complementary action on prices would not be possible. They were sufficiently persuasive for the policy to be accepted at that level and a week later the General Council voted narrowly by 19 votes to 13 to support the £6 a week norm. The General Council also stipulated that those earning above £7,000 per annum should obtain no increase at all and that the flat rate should be payable as a bonus and be the only increase permitted during the next twelve-month period (in an effort to minimize wage drift). On 11 July the government released a White Paper, *The Attack on Inflation*,[12] which basically endorsed the TUC's wage guidelines, although it raised the cut-off point for wage increases to £8,500 and called the £6 a maximum obtainable, rather than a universal, entitlement. The government also outlined the measures it intended to take to enforce compliance. Price controls would be used to prevent private sector employers from passing on the costs of excessive wage increases. In the public sector cash limits for expenditure programmes were introduced early in 1976 to perform a similar function: if there was widespread non-compliance legislation would be introduced to legally forbid employers to grant increases above £6. Food subsidies would be extended to limit the inflation of certain prices to less than 10 per cent. Rent increases would be held to the rate of inflation.

The legislation to back the policy up was only passed because of Conservative abstention. Thirty Labour MPs also abstained. The policy was approved at the TUC Annual Conference by a majority of 2:1, not least because it was recognized that Britain's economic performance was continuing to deteriorate, and also because of extensive lobbying by Len Murray and Jack Jones. The government launched a massive publicity campaign to encourage compliance and TUC officials kept a very close eye on developments. It soon became obvious that the rank and file had indeed grasped the extent of Britain's economic ills and that the policy was holding. The inflation of basic wage rates came down from an annual figure of 33.1 per cent in the second quarter of 1975 to 18.7 per cent in the third quarter of 1976. Over the same period price inflation tumbled from 26.6 per cent to 13.7 per cent. While part of this was the result of Healey's tighter monetary and fiscal stance in 1975, such a large drop would have been unlikely in the absence of the pay limit.

III
Social Contract Part III: 1976–7

Soon after the TUC Annual Conference the trade union leaders began to consider what should happen in the next pay round. The major question was whether or not the subsequent phase of incomes policy should again operate on a flat-rate basis, as mooted by Jack Jones, or on a percentage norm basis with a view to restoring differentials. In

January Denis Healey opened up discussions with the General Council about the 1976–7 wage round and made it clear that the government would not accept another flat-rate norm. Healey also sought to tempt the trade unions into greater restraint by offering the incentive of tax cuts in the 1976 budget. The General Council would not, however, be drawn into a pre-budget agreement and so in his budget speech Healey announced his intention to introduce across-the-board tax reductions worth more than £1,200 million, but that only £300 million of these would be granted unconditionally. The whole package would only be introduced if the TUC agreed to try to restrict wage increases to 3 per cent over the next year. Higher trade union wage guidelines would yield prospectively less in the way of tax relief.

This was the first budget in British history the implementation of which was contingent on the whims of an extra-parliamentary body. Not surprisingly many outside commentators characterized it as 'taxation without representation'. *The Times* for one suggested that the budget had actually transformed the TUC into a sort of 'Second House of Parliament, a second chamber with power and authority the House of Lords has long since lost'. This was portrayed as a defeat for democracy as the TUC represented only a limited constituency.[13] The budget was also a new departure for the 'Social Contract'. In offering tax cuts in exchange for wage restraint rather than improvements in the 'social wage' through economic and social reform, the government had resorted to a much more direct method of securing wage restraint, and one which appealed to the self-interest of the wage earner rather than more idealistic sentiments.

Throughout April and early May the Chancellor and the TUC's NEDC representatives sought to reach agreement on a wage restraint package. The TUC wanted at least a 5 per cent wage norm plus all the tax relief, but Healey ruled that out as too extravagant. Finally it took the development of another sterling crisis consequent on an effort to stimulate the economy via an engineered devaluation of the exchange rate, together with threats to call an election, to convince the unions of the need for a more responsible attitude. The terms finally agreed were a 5 per cent increase for those earning at or near the national average, increases of at least £2.50, or more than 5 per cent, for those earning less than £50 a week, and increases no greater than 4 per cent for those earning more than £80 a week. The average wage increase was expected to be around 4.5 per cent and the average earnings increase some 6.5 to 7 per cent. As the unions did not insist on any special cases or loopholes, the government decided to grant all the tax concessions originally proposed. The General Council this time approved the package by 25 votes to 5, and the government released a second White Paper on pay restraint entitled *The Attack on Inflation – The Second Year*.[14] One union after another pledged its support for the policy, although most warned that this would have to be the last round of formal restraint. The call was for an orderly return to free collective bargaining in August 1977.

IV
The IMF Crisis

To stabilize sterling during the exchange crisis of the early summer of 1976, a central bank loan of some $5.3 billion was negotiated. In return, Healey sought to restore confidence in the currency by trimming £1 billion off public expenditure in 1977–8 and by adding 2 per cent to employers' National Insurance contributions to yield a further £1 billion in a full year. In addition interest rates were raised and a target for monetary growth (M3) of 12 per cent was announced for 1976–7, with a view to influencing the inflationary expectations of unions, employers and financial markets alike. The implication was that excessive wage claims would not be accommodated, they would merely add to the dole queues. These measures were perceived by international financial opinion as too little, too late. The Americans in particular remained convinced that Britain was living far beyond its means. Sterling soon began to slide again and, with no more central bank credits available, the government pushed interest rates up to an all-time high and sought a conditional IMF loan which would require the inspection of the nation's finances. New Prime Minister James Callaghan also made a speech to the Labour Party Conference in which he appeared to abandon formally the use of expansionary fiscal policy to maintain full employment because of its propensity to produce accelerating inflation. In reality, as we have noted, the end of the full employment era had been signalled by the budget of 1975; what this statement really sought to do was signal to the financial markets that Britain had now most definitely changed economic course.

The IMF eventually granted Britain a massive loan of $3.9 billion in return for public expenditure economies designed to effect a £3 billion reduction in the Public Sector Borrowing Requirement over the next two years, and a commitment to direct tax reductions and a declining target path for domestic credit expansion over the period to 1979. Negotiations were close to breakdown on several occasions as the IMF sought to impose more drastic cuts on the government. There were echoes of the exchange crisis of 1931 as the Cabinet divided over acceptance of the IMF's terms, or the resort to alternative strategies, including one to retreat into a highly controlled 'siege economy'. In the end, however, a compromise was reached, although not before both Healey and Callaghan had come close to the end of their tethers. During 1977 the pound made a remarkable recovery.

V
The Social Contract Part IV: 1977–8

By the middle of 1977, assisted by tight monetary and fiscal policies and the escalation of unemployment to 1.3 million, the earnings index was rising at an annual rate of some 8.5 per cent. While this represented a higher rate than was hoped for, it was considerably lower than a year before. The seemingly obvious success of the incomes policies of 1975–6 and 1976–7 in reducing the growth of earnings led to considerable discussion in some quarters about long-run, or even permanent, wage restraint. Indeed as early as the end of 1975, the Chancellor himself was already talking of moving towards what 'has been achieved in other countries [where] ordinary working people and their representatives sit down at the beginning of the year with the government, discuss what is likely to happen to the economy during the year, decide broadly speaking what sort of wage increases will make sense given the other claims of the economy, and then try voluntarily to limit their claims during the year to that broad limit'.[15] The TUC for its part never gave any indication that it would support wage restraint other than as a purely temporary expedient. That such hopes for long-term incomes policy were merely wishful thinking was soon made apparent to the government when it sought to press the General Council to develop a further restraint formula in anticipation of the 1977–8 wage round. Widespread and vocal opposition to such a policy soon emerged throughout the union movement. A 40 per cent depreciation in sterling during 1976 had caused import prices to explode and price inflation to move above 16 per cent per annum in the first half of 1977 at the same time as earnings were growing much more slowly. By the end of the

1976–7 wage round average real earnings had fallen by over 7 per cent. Furthermore, there was again considerable pressure at this stage from skilled workers seeking to ensure that their differentials were maintained. Union leaders themselves were split as to what policy to follow. Jack Jones and David Basnett of the General and Municipal Workers' Union (GMWU) argued that it would be foolish to relinquish the gains of the last two years by a return to the law of the jungle. Others like Joe Gormley (NUM) looked at rank and file sentiment and concluded that to try to impose further formal restraint was impracticable.

Nevertheless, in the 1977 budget the government offered to reduce the basic rate of income tax by 2 per cent in return for a wage restraint deal. In conjunction with unconditional tax reductions this would yield an average increase in 'take home' pay of some 4.5 per cent. Later the TUC General Council was told that the overall growth of earnings had to be restricted to 10 per cent if inflation was to be in single figures in 1978, so if scope was to be allowed for special cases to improve differentials, general wage increases would have to be around 4 or 5 per cent over the next wage round. The TUC leadership was not impressed. Its members thought that the government was expecting too much of them, while they also wanted the budget to be more reflationary. The income tax concessions offered were offset by higher indirect taxes, while the government's hands were tied on social expenditure by its promises to the IMF. Moreover, the tax cuts of 1976 had in reality only partially offset the effects of fiscal drag for the average wage earner. The government was also unwilling to do anything substantial about price control.

Bipartite discussions continued through the early summer of 1977 without a breakthrough. The TUC told ministers that any wage norm which, allowing for the proposed tax concessions, did not at least compensate for the rise in the cost of living during the 1976–7 wage round (that is, 10 to 12 per cent) would stand no chance of holding. This was unacceptable to the government. Jones and Murray then sought a compromise whereby the trade union leadership would agree to support the twelve-month rule and to seek to influence wage bargaining without any talk of norms or guidelines. This package was also turned down by ministers at the beginning of July, although both Foot and Tony Benn supported it in Cabinet. The government decided instead to impose more formal wage restraint unilaterally and issued a White Paper announcing its intent to keep the overall rise in earnings to 10 per cent over the coming wage round. Basic wage increases were to

111

be limited to one a year and to be 'well within single figures'. Only genuine productivity agreements would be allowed to breach this limit. The government also announced a number of powers with which it hoped to enforce the policy. It would refuse to give permission to companies seeking price increases in violation of the twelve-month rule; it would trim or curtail state purchases from firms granting excessive wage increases; cash limits would be rigidly maintained and only half the proposed income tax reduction would be granted.[16]

When the July White Paper was published, the government warned the TUC that a policy of concerted opposition would force it to resign. The trade union leadership's reaction to the document was muted; it wanted to help the government as much as possible. After the introduction of local incentive schemes allowed the NCB to grant the miners a basic settlement of 10 per cent in early 1978, and the failure of a firemen's strike to breach the guideline, one group after another reached agreement just within the scope offered in the government policy. The problem was, however, that in many cases this was accomplished only with the promise of a more substantial settlement in the next pay round; and only after the negotiation of an additional, frequently bogus, productivity deal. While in the period mid 1977 to mid 1978 price inflation fell from an annual rate of 16.5 per cent to 7.7 per cent as sterling appreciated and the previous year's wage restraint exerted an effect on prices, over the same period wages and earnings inflation bounced back to 15 and 17 per cent respectively.

V
The Social Contract Part V:
1978–9, and the
'Winter of Discontent'

When the 1978 wage round appeared on the horizon the government made no real effort to reach a voluntary agreement with the TUC at all, it merely sought to discuss the details of a new compulsory policy. The government, urged on by the Prime Minister, decided to go this time for a very restrictive 5 per cent ceiling on any group's total earnings in an effort to present itself to the electorate as determined inflation-fighters in the run-up to the next election, expected in the autumn. The government substantiated its case for a restrictive norm by pointing to the 8 per cent growth in average real earnings in the previous wage round. The only exceptions were to be for self-financing productivity deals and for those earning less than £44.50 for a normal working week.[17] The government tried hard to enlist the TUC's support for the policy, but the 1978 Annual TUC Conference passed overwhelmingly a resolution rejecting stage IV. Callaghan had by this time decided against an autumn election and so had committed the government to enforcing the policy rigidly throughout the wage round if it was to be taken seriously when going to the country in the following year.

Stage IV was soon being challenged. Faced with a 5 per cent pay offer, the workers at Ford mounted an unofficial strike which rapidly became official. Ford raised its pay offer successively until the workforce settled for an increase of over 17 per cent. The government announced that it would impose the rather ineffective sanction of refusing to buy Ford cars in the hope that companies with more to lose from breaking the incomes policy guidelines would take heed. However, before the government could introduce these constitutionally dubious sanctions (dubious in the sense that they involved the imposition of state sanctions without legislation to back them up), the House of Commons voted to support a Conservative-sponsored resolution condemning them. A number of left-wing Labour MPs had abstained and thus the government was forced to announce that it would no longer utilize this weapon. Furthermore, as Peter Shore, the Trade and Industry Secretary, emphasized to the Cabinet, the end of sanctions also signalled the end of the government's moral authority in the restriction of public sector pay.[18] This episode was followed by a number of serious industrial disputes by which a variety of groups including the tanker drivers, lorry drivers, ambulancemen, hospital workers, sanitation workers, local authority manual workers and train drivers sought to breach the pay guidelines. The year 1979 was to see 29 million working days lost to strike action, the worst twelve-month record in the postwar period. The inconvenience to the public during what became known as the 'Winter of Discontent' was enormous, and many, including a significantly number of Labour Cabinet ministers, were disgusted at the seemingly selfish, uncaring and bloody-minded methods many workers were using to pursue wage claims.

It soon became clear that stage IV had to be amended. Some members of the Cabinet wanted to raise the norm, while others called for a 'freeze'. As Joel Barnett has put it, 'whilst many recognized that a freeze might ultimately become necessary, it was not [in January and February 1979] a practical proposition, nor could it be done by a government without a majority to carry it through the House' (by-elections had deprived Labour of its overall majority).[19] Thus the government raised the pay norm to what was effectively 9 per cent. Additionally in February 1979, and after intense discussions, the government and the unions jointly issued a statement under the title *The Economy, the Government and Trade Union Responsibility*, which attempted re-establishing public confidence in the ability of the government to work with the unions and keep industrial relations and inflation under control. The 'Concordat', as it was known, recognized that the 5 per cent norm had been a failure, set a target of the reduction of inflation to below 5 per cent by 1982, pronounced the establishment of an independent committee to investigate pay comparability between the private and public sectors, and elicited promises from the trade unions of fewer strikes, less picketing and looser closed shops.

VII
Conclusions

Despite the new pact with the trade unions, the fact that inflation was kept in single figures in the first half of 1979, and the engineering of a mini-boom which brought unemployment down slightly to 1.2 million, Labour lost the election of May 1979. It can be argued convincingly that, as with the Heath government before it, difficulties in respect to wage policy played a considerable part in the demise of the Wilson–Callaghan government. After a disastrous beginning, for two years, aided by the deflation which reduced the scope for wage drift and raised unemployment, incomes policy was successful. Thereafter, it became increasingly ineffective and unpopular until the 'Winter of Discontent' turned the public violently against Labour and its interventionist and corporalist approach to economic policy-making. Anti-union feeling was at an all-time high in 1979. The electorate was ready for a more simplistic, *laissez-faire* approach to the control of inflation and the nation's economic ills as preached by the Tories. Ten years of trade unionists trooping into No. 10 Downing Street for beer, sandwiches and a chat about wage restraint had not in the eye of the average voter produced very satisfactory results. Inflation was still unacceptably high and considered endemic, unemployment had risen to levels unheard of since the 1930s, Britain had recently been forced to go cap in hand to the IMF, and most importantly, industrial unrest was rife. But for all this, one must question what would have been the outcome had Callaghan decided to go to the country in the previous autumn? At that stage Labour's economic policies looked much more credible and in hindsight we can say that the government would have stood a much better chance of re-election. As Joel Barnett has put it, 'Jim Callaghan certainly did not anticipate just how rough the winter would be when he made his fateful decision to postpone the election'.[20]

Part of Conservative propaganda during the run-up to the 1979 election was the assertion that the TUC had effectively been running the country for most of the previous five years; such a statement deserves attention, if only to expose it as the misrepresentation it was. It is true that in its first year in office the Labour government introduced a wide range of policies which had been sought by the TUC, but many of these had been developed independently within the Labour Party's NEC when it had a left-wing majority. Thereafter, as the economic crisis deepened, and the moderates in the Cabinet and within the party as a whole asserted themselves, while they continued to take the trade unions into their confidence, the government ignored or rejected a large number of TUC proposals for further extensions of state intervention and control, and withdrew or watered down many of the concessions it had made originally to trade union opinion. This particularly applies to its policies pertaining to industrial democracy, industrial planning and support, income distribution and price control. Furthermore, in mid 1976 the government introduced the first of what was to become a series of annual targets for money supply growth.

The Chancellor explicitly warned the unions that he would not amend these targets to accommodate wage inflation. Increased union militancy would merely lead to unemployment. But most importantly of all, and to the absolute dismay of the trade unions, the commitment to full employment as it had existed throughout the postwar era was effectively suspended in April 1975. In the following years, despite repeated calls from the TUC for major and sustained reflationary action, the government's fiscal policy remained cautious. The growth of public expenditure was sharply restrained, and the PSBR strictly limited, as is illustrated in Tables 8.2 and 8.3.

Despite the government's promise prior to the October 1974 election that the 'Social Contract' was 'at the heart' of its plans to save the nation, as originally propounded, it was effectively dead by April 1975. Thus while it would be fair to say that the Wilson–Callaghan government offered the trade unions opportunities to broaden their

Table 8.2   *Public Expenditure at Constant Prices as a Percentage of GDP, 1973–9*

1973–4	39.9
1974–5	45.0
1975–6	45.4
1976–7	43.0
1977–8	39.3
1978–9	40.4

Source: Sir Leo Pliatzky, *Getting and Spending. Public Expenditure, Employment and Inflation* (Oxford: Blackwell, 1982), p. 218.

influence on economic policy, it can hardly be said that the latter were allowed to dominate the former's decision-making.

The effective abandonment of full employment as a short-term aim and the introduction of monetary growth targets in 1975 and 1976 have been seen as marking the beginning of the monetarist era in the United Kingdom. This judgement needs some qualification too. Labour travelled nowhere near as far down the monetarist road as its Conservative successors. Under Labour, while monetary targeting came to have a role to play, it was only one policy lever amongst many, and it was by no means the pivotal lever. What is more, monetarist theory was never wholeheartedly embraced; the emphasis under Labour, despite the 1975 budget and Callaghan's speech to the 1976 Labour Party Conference, was still on short-run demand management and stabilization policy rather than the creation of a stable long-term macroeconomic environment through strict monetary guidelines. As such, the approach remained broadly Keynesian, it merely recognized

Table 8.3   *Public Sector Borrowing Requirement 1972–9*

	£ms at constant prices	As percentage of GDP
1972	2,039	3.66
1973	4,198	6.48
1974	6,365	8.47
1975	10,477	11.03
1976	9,144	8.12
1977	5,975	4.67
1978	8,335	5.66
1979	12.638	7.47

Source: Central Statistical Office, *Economic Trends* (London: HMSO).

the need to take control of the money supply more seriously than had been the case under previous postwar governments, the constraints imposed upon policy-makers by the inflationary circumstances of the time, the difficulties a single nation faces when reflating alone, and the perceptions of financial markets. It was only with the arrival of Mrs Thatcher that the Keynesian era in the United Kingdom was closed.

9

The Era of Thatcherism 1979–

I

Monetarism and the Tories

While the Conservatives were in opposition during the 1970s the balance of power in the party shifted to the right. Under Margaret Thatcher's leadership, the party, no doubt mindful of the economic débâcle of 1972–4, rejected the Keynesian interventionist economic policies of Edward Heath's premiership and the traditionally practical approach of the Tories and came to embrace the monetarist free market doctrines of economists such as Milton Friedman. In the words of Sir Leo Pliatzky, 'the Conservative victory in May 1979 was more than just another change of government; in terms of political and economic philosophy it was a revolution'.[1]

Monetarists, in contrast to Keynes, believe in a stable or predictable velocity of circulation and thus that the growth of money national income can usually be reasonably well explained by the rate of growth of the money stock. Thus the central feature of monetarist thinking is the strict control of the supply of money. When there is a change in the growth of money national income as a result of a change in the rate of growth of money supply the initial effect will be 'real' or on output, but soon after, the effect will be increasingly on prices, until within a period of about two years, this secondary effect absorbs the whole of the increase in the money supply and output returns to its original level. Budgetary policy *per se* can only affect output in the short run. If a fiscal adjustment is associated with a change in monetary growth then there will be a 'real effect', but in the long run the effect will be on the price level. If a fiscal adjustment is made with no accompanying change in monetary growth, the effect of the policy shock on demand and prices will merely 'crowd out' a compensatory amount of private sector demand through the effects of an increasing demand for money on interest rates and in turn the exchange rate. Although the centrepiece of macroeconomic policy must therefore be the rate of growth of the money supply, this lever should not be used for discretionary short-run stabilization policy because of the long and variable lags in the effects of money on the economy, and as governments within a democratic context are not to be trusted in prognosis or policy adjustment. Instead the government should set in advance and publish a steady growth path for the money supply to reduce uncertainty and to guide all economic agents in their decisions.

As far as the labour market is concerned, monetarists emphasize the concept of the 'natural rate of unemployment'. They believe that at this level of unemployment, set by institutional factors and the individual characteristics of the labour market in any given country, there is a constraint rate of inflation. Unemployment below the 'natural rate' can only be maintained at the cost of steadily accelerating inflation, indeed the acceleration of the inflation rate is the very cause of lower unemployment as it leads to workers overestimating their future real wage levels and finding the prospect of employment more attractive. By the same token, a deceleration of inflation has the opposite effect and produces unemployment above the 'natural rate'. It is only when inflation and inflationary expectations are matched that unemployment will be at its 'natural rate'. All unemployment above the 'natural rate' is defined by monetarists as 'voluntary' as it arises from workers' unwillingness to accept work at the market-clearing wage. Unemployment is not caused by demand deficiency but is the result of an interplay between actual prices (which of course are affected by demand) and expected prices.

A pure monetarist approach to the economy also implies that there is no role for incomes policy. It is seen as an irrelevancy since inflation can be controlled effectively enough by monetary discipline. It is also viewed as an example of excessive government intervention leading to a loss of freedom and liberty, while by distorting differentials it reduces market efficiency and actually raises unemployment. In short monetarists believe that governments cause inflation, not unions. All unions can do is price people out of jobs by forcing up wages above the market clearing level through their monopoly power. To reduce unemployment the monopoly power of the unions should be tackled by legislation designed to increase competition in the labour market, not by direct controls. Under a monetarist regime, employment policy, and indeed growth policy, becomes essentially microeconomic, operating through "supply side', while counter-inflation policy is macroeconomic. This, of course, is the reverse of the role-playing which characterized the Keynesian era of policy-making.

How then has this theory been translated into economic policy in the six years from 1979 to 1985 and what has been the result? Since coming to power the Conservatives have indeed pursued two aims consistent with the monetarist approach: the reduction of inflation via monetary policy, and the improvement of the economy's employment and growth performance through the liberalization of markets, income tax concessions and the rolling back of the frontiers of the state. Full employment as an explicit target has been abandoned and the commitment embodied in the 1944 *Employment Policy* White Paper cast aside. Nigel Lawson, Chancellor of the Exchequer at the time of writing (1985), has described present-day Conservative economic policy as follows:

The British Experiment ... consists of seeking within an explicit medium-term context to provide increasing freedom for markets to work within a framework of firm monetary and financial discipline. The traditional assignment of policies to targets, namely macroeconomic policy being primarily used to promote the growth of output and employment, and microeconomic policy being used to control inflation, has been reversed. The new approach relies on macroeconomic policy to reduce inflation and to provide a consistent framework for the overall expansion of nominal income, while microeconomic policy is used to create conditions conducive to growth and employment.[2]

Formal incomes policy has indeed been completely ignored, although the government has from late 1980 taken a particularly hard line on public sector pay, and has tried constantly to talk down pay settlements in the private sector and make the trade unions bargain more responsibly. Thus the Treasury and Civil Service Committee set up to monitor macroeconomic policy on behalf of Parliament was told that

the Government have ... eschewed all the apparatus of formal incomes policies which have failed in the past and led to distortion in the labour market ... the Government do not intend to intervene in individual wage negotiations except where they are inevitably involved as direct employers.[3]

In the Conservatives' first budget, presented soon after the 1979 election, the then Chancellor, Sir Geoffrey Howe, replaced Denis Healey's monetary target of 8–12 per cent growth in M3 with one of 9 per cent and cut government expenditure by £3.5 billion and income tax by £4.5 billion. To recoup the revenue lost by this action he was also forced to raise VAT from 8 per cent to 15 per cent and to remove the subsidies from nationalized industry prices. By doing so he raised the retail price index by 4 per cent and added enormously to inflationary expectations at a time when the government sought to do the opposite. Moreover, during the election campaign the Tories made the rather rash and expensive promise to honour the recommendations of the Clegg Commission on public sector pay, which was set up to sort out the chaos created by the breakdown of Labour's 5 per cent pay policy. At a time when public sector cash limits were fixed to allow for pay rises of 5 per cent, the Clegg Commission's findings resulted in an increase of 25 per cent in the public sector wage bill in twelve months. In the private sector, negotiators, rather than basing their claims on the scope provided by the government's monetary target, sought to keep up with the going rate established in the public sector. The result was an upsurge in inflation and the onset of an unprecedented fall in output and rise in unemployment. A year after coming to power on the back of promises to eradicate inflation and put Britain back to work, the Conservatives were presiding over an inflation rate of more than 21 per cent and unemployment approaching 1.5 million.

Undaunted by all this, the government continued to preach the gospel of monetarism with missionary zeal. In the 1980 budget Howe introduced a four-year Medium Term Financial Strategy (MTFS) to generate favourable expectations and to provide a consistent framework for macroeconomic policy through the linking of monetary and fiscal policy target paths. This new departure in economic policy-making was forced through by the Chief Economic Adviser Terry Burns and the then Financial Secretary to the Treasury, Nigel Lawson, despite the considerable scepticism of many of the practical men within the Treasury and the Bank of England who did not wish to be committed so firmly and so far ahead, and who wondered what all this would mean to the man in the street. The MTFS mapped out a steady reduction in the growth of nominal incomes with price stability as its ultimate goal. At the same time it represented rather than a willingness to unbalance the budget to stabilize output, a plan to balance the budget on an inflation-adjusted basis. It deliberately ruled out the operation of fiscal stabilizers intended in the Keynesian era to reduce short-term fluctuations in economic activity. Fiscal policy would only be adjusted to help meet monetary targets as the PSBR was seen as the major determinant of monetary growth.

121

Table 9.1A *MTFS Projections and Outturns*

	Money supply M3 percentage change per annum									
	1979–80	*1980–81*	*1981–2*	*1982–3*	*1983–4*	*1984–5*	*1985–6*	*1986–7*	*1987–8*	*1988–9*
June 1979	9									
March 1980		7–11								
March 1981			6–10	5–9	4–8					
March 1982			6–10	5–9	4–8	6–10				
March 1983				8–12	7–11	6–10	5–9			
March 1984					7–11	6–10	5–9	4–8	3–7	2–6
March 1985						6–10	5–9	4–8	3–7	2–6
Actual (Seasonally Adjusted)	11.2	19.4	12.8	11.2	10.1	8.5	12.33			

N.B. From the start of the financial year 1984–5 sterling M3 was redefined to exclude public sector bank deposits. Figures here are on the old basis until March 1984. Actual figure for 1985–6 relates to first six months only.

Sources: Central Statistical Office, *Economic Trends* (London: HMSO).
OECD, *United Kingdom Economic Survey* (Paris: OECD, 1985).

Table 9.1B Public Sector Borrowing Requirement as Percentage of GDP

	1979–80	1980–81	1981–2	1982–3	1983–4	1984–5	1985–6	1986–7	1987–8	1988–9
June 1979	4.5									
March 1980	4.75	3.75								
March 1981	5	6	3	2.25	1.5					
March 1982		5.7	4.25	3.25	2	2				
March 1983			4.25	3.5	2.75	2.5	2			
March 1984			3.5	2.75	2.75	2.25	2	2	1.75	1.75
March 1985				3.3	3.25		2	2	1.33	1.75
Actual	4.9	5.7	3.4	3.3	3.25	3.25				
Actual (£ billion)	9.9	13.2	8.7	9.2	10.1	10.5				

Sources: Central Statistical Office, Economic Trends (London: HMSO)
Fiscal Studies, vol. 6, no. 2, May 1985
OECD, United Kingdom Economic Survey (Paris: OECD, 1985).

The MTFS remains in place today (1985), although it has undergone a number of changes in the projected paths of the intermediate targets. Initially there were enormous difficulties in hitting the target paths for both monetary and fiscal policy, resulting in a major regearing in 1982. All in all alterations to the monetary aggregates targeted have been made three times. In the 1982 budget a narrower measure of money, M1, was introduced together with a broader measure, PSL2. In the 1984 budget the targets for M1 and PSL2 were dropped and replaced by a target for the narrow monetary base, M0.[4] In October 1985 M3, formerly the only indicator of monetary policy to have been targeted in every year since the inception of the MTFS, was temporarily dropped, leaving only M0 as an official target, although for some time before this the strength of the exchange rate, the trend of Money GDP and the actual inflation rate had been adopted as guides to monetary conditions. While at the time of the publication of the initial MTFS in 1980 it was stated that the way the money supply was defined for target purposes might need to be adjusted now and then as circumstances change, the fact that each time a target has been dropped it has been growing well outside its target range has tended to increase outsiders' scepticism about the MTFS, which appears to have been modified to fit the facts. Moreover, the suspension of a target for M3, for the sake of which, in 1980 and 1981, interest rates and sterling were allowed to rise to record levels, has an irony all of its own.

As far as the 'supply side' of the economy is concerned, the government has *inter alia* acted on several points to make the labour market more conducive to market forces and to adjust real wages more rapidly to their market clearing level. Basically, this has involved efforts to change the legal framework of industrial relations, and in particular efforts to curb the powers of the trade unions and to remove some of the legal immunities introduced during the Wilson–Callaghan years. The Employment Acts of 1980 and 1982 and the Trade Union Act of 1984 have led to the removal of legal immunities for picketing other than by employees at their place of work, and for secondary industrial action; introduction and strengthening of rights for employees dismissed for refusing to join closed shops; the institution of secret ballots to approve new closed shops and to confirm previous closed shops; the removal of legal immunities from civil actions so as to make trade unions subject to injunctions and damages when they are responsible for unlawful industrial action; the removal of legal immunities from civil actions in any industrial dispute which has not been

124

agreed in advance by a secret ballot of the membership, and the stipulation that executive committees of trade unions be elected by secret ballot at least every five years. In addition the Conservatives have endeavoured to improve work incentives and labour mobility through lower income tax and social security benefits and by improving industrial training. Furthermore, the government is now seeking to remove the artificially created wage floors set by wages councils for 2.75 million workers in twenty-six industries because this system 'impedes the freedom of employers to offer, and job seekers to take, jobs at wages that would otherwise be acceptable and so restricts job opportunities, particularly for the young'.[5]

II
The Results of the 'Thatcher Experiment'

What then have been the results of this experiment in economic policy-making? The first point to make is that the government succeeded in bringing down price inflation from a peak of over 20 per cent in 1980 (for which in many ways it had itself to blame) to below 5 per cent in 1983. However, no real progress has been made since. The major aim of the government's strategy has been to a large extent achieved, but one must question whether the end result actually justifies the means employed and how permanent the reduction in inflation will be. The defeat of inflation might yet prove itself to be only temporary, and has only been achieved at a massive cost in terms of unemployment, and a marked deterioration in labour market conditions. As Table 9.2 shows, we are now a long way from the full employment era of the 1940s, 1950s and 1960s.

While part of the deterioration in labour market conditions from 1979 to 1985 can be ascribed to the second OPEC price shock, world recession and demographical factors, much must be seen as the result of the Conservative government's extreme disinflationary measures wedded to wage and price inflexibility. In the months after the announcement of the MTFS, the Clegg Commission awards and the increases in VAT and nationalized industry prices continued to exert upward pressure on the retail price index and on the demand for money to finance a given number of transactions. Given the strong demand for money, the restrictive targets for the money supply led to strong upward pressure on interest rates. The high interest rates, added to

Table 9.2   *Labour Market Conditions 1979–84*

	1979	1980	1981	1982	1983	1984(1)	1984(2)	1984(3)
Working population (percentage change from previous period, seasonally adjusted)	0.9	0.7	0.0	0.0	0.3	1.3	0.7	
Total in employment (percentage change from previous period, seasonally adjusted)	1.3	−1.0	−3.4	−1.5	−0.4	0.6	0.5	
Number unemployed (in thousands, excluding school-leavers)	1,227	1,561	2,419	2,793	2,970	2,998	3,026	3,076
Unemployment rate	5.1	6.4	9.9	11.5	12.3	12.5	12.6	12.8
Unlisted vacancies (in thousands)	241	143	97	111	145	147	154	166
Retail prices	15.0	18.0	11.9	8.6	4.6	5.2	5.1	4.7
Average earnings	20.2	12.9	9.4	8.4	8.0	6.1	5.4	

Source: OECD, *United Kingdom Economic Survey* (Paris: OECD, 1985)

sterling's petro-currency status and the confidence of financial markets in the success of Mrs Thatcher's strategy, forced the exchange rate ever higher and rendered British goods grossly uncompetitive. Early in 1979 the rate was \$2.00 = £1.00. In the third quarter of 1980 the rate was \$2.40 = £1.00. The index of Britain's real exchange rate (the average exchange rate adjusted for inflation) rose from 106.3 in 1978 (1973 = 100) to 118.4 in 1979, 137.9 in 1980 and over 140 in mid 1981. In contrast the indices for France and West Germany, two major competitors, hardly changed at all over the same period. Dr Otmar Emminger, former president of the West German Bundesbank, told a House of Commons Select Committee on the Treasury that the rise in sterling's real exchange rate was 'by far the most excessive over-valuation which any major currency has experienced in recent monetary history'.[6] While the rise in the exchange rate together with the monetary and fiscal squeeze and a sharp fall in world commodity prices helped to bring down Britain's inflation rate from mid 1980, it crippled British industry and forced a massive labour shake-out and precipitous

Table 9.3   GDP at Constant Factor Cost (percentage change over
previous year)

1979	+2.9
1980	−3.3
1981	−2.1
1982	+1.5

fall-off in economic activity unlike anything seen in the United Kingdom since the Great Depression, and much worse than anything experienced abroad. The Tory policies had been much too severe.

Ironically, what was also symptomatic of the Thatcher government's MTFS was that, rather than holding the money supply within a preannounced target range, it actually tended to swell the money supply figures because of so-called 'distress borrowing'. Companies were increasing their demands for loans to keep afloat. The use of high interest rates to reduce monetary growth was actually causing companies to borrow more to meet the increased cost of existing loans and thus increasing the growth of the money supply. Thus the idea that the PSBR was the key element in control of the money supply and interest rates (and indeed that the money supply determined the rate of inflation) became subject to considerable doubt. In 1979, 1980 and 1981, the PSBR contributed a very minor role to changes in the money supply, while in contrast private sector borrowing very nearly equalled the growth in money supply in 1980, and in 1979 and 1981 exceeded it by a substantial margin. It should also be noted that once the government began to fail to hit its money-supply targets, the job of bringing monetary growth back within the derived range became increasingly harder. As the targets were exceeded, the financial markets expected a rise in interest rates and would not buy gilts. When interest rates were raised, this caused more distress borrowing and more monetary growth and worsened the monetary overshoot. The first year of the MTFS saw M3 growing at an annual rate of 19.4 per cent, which was more than twice the midpoint of the target range of 7–11 per cent, and the overshoot in 1981–2 was little better.

As far as interest rate policy was concerned, the success of monetary targeting was given less weight than the anguished cries of industry in 1981, and in the 1982 budget the government's MTFS was comprehensively regeared and other monetary measures in addition to sterling M3 were adopted. In the financial years 1982–3, 1983–4 and

127

1984–5, sterling M3 grew within its allotted range. Although fiscal policy remained extremely tight and there was no traditional reflation, a recovery was under way by late 1981. Consumer spending was stimulated by an upsurge in real wages as price inflation fell faster than the rate of growth of earnings, a fall in the savings ratio and the abolition of hire purchase controls. This recovery has continued steadily if unspectacularly to the present (1985) and has broadened into exports and investment as President Reagan's reflationary policies fuelled a world boom. The average growth rate since 1979, however, remains a mere 1 per cent, the lowest figure for any such period since the Second World War. Moreover, almost half of the United Kingdom's growth since 1979 is accounted for by the boom in North Sea oil production. This has given jobs to a mere 80,000 people, against the 2 million lost elsewhere in the economy. Consistent growth has done nothing to prevent a continued escalation of unemployment, which at the time of writing (1985) represents over 13 per cent of the workforce on the basis of government figures.

The government has put the blame for the continued rise in unemployment on the trade unions for keeping pay levels at too high a level. Average earnings have continued to increase at an annual rate of around 8 per cent, even though there is an enormous amount of slack in the labour market by the standards of earlier postwar decades, and prices have been rising by 3 or 4 points less. In its second period of office, conscious of its failures with respect to jobs and wages, the government has announced its intentions to move ahead more rapidly with supply-side measures such as the abolition of wages councils, and the removal of the 'poverty trap' to help reduce wage claims and improve the division of national income between prices and output. In March 1985, it released its own monetarist White Paper on employment policy, entitled *Employment. The Challenge for the Nation*, which suggested that

jobs will be created to the extent that people are prepared to work at wages that employers can afford. Over the past four years the economy has been steadily growing. But too much of the benefit of that economic growth has gone in higher pay for those in work at the expense of those without jobs.

It added that employment could increase considerably if people accepted slightly lower earnings growth, but rejected outright government-imposed pay policies as 'the cycle of distortion, pent-up pressure and explosion is painfully proven'.[7]

While seeking to reduce the monopolistic immunities and privileges enjoyed by the trade union movement as a whole has something to be said for it as a means to reduce general pressure on pay, the problem with the government's approach is that its recent pronouncements have focused on the low paid and the special need for them to price themselves into jobs. The government seems to have looked at the growth in aggregate earnings and concluded that since the unskilled and low paid have been hit hardest by unemployment, their wage claims are the ones that most need to be scaled down. Recent policies have, therefore, been designed to free the labour market at the lower end. Disaggregated figures on pay suggest, however, that the wage problem in recent years has been most pronounced at the top end of the income distribution and that therefore the rich have actually priced the poor out of jobs. The policy of attacking the low paid is misguided and grossly unfair. The top 10 per cent of full-time adult male wage earners increased their real gross earnings (after allowing for price increases) by 19 per cent between April 1979 and April 1984, while the bottom 10 per cent actually took a real earnings cut of 0.2 per cent over the same period. Increases in real earnings under Mrs Thatcher's government have actually been progressively larger, the higher up the income distribution a worker finds himself.

The fact is that today in many parts of the labour market in the United Kingdom, employers and unions fix wages without much regard to market conditions, as a form of insurance. If the market deteriorates some workers only are laid off and the majority do not take lower pay increases. This is because it is known that the people who are going to be laid off will be those hired last, or those who are due to retire. Workforces tend to be divided into 'insiders' whose jobs are rarely at risk and 'outsiders' whose jobs are. The 'outsiders' tend to be the young and the unskilled. The government's proposed legislation in the labour market seems to be attacking the already beleaguered and hard-hit 'outsiders'. The real task for the government, as it has been for all governments since the war, is to make all workers limit their wage increases, 'insiders' and 'outsiders', rich and poor. One is hard pressed to find a really fair solution for effectively restricting *all* wage and salary increases without returning to the idea of some form of formal incomes policy.

By any set of objective criteria the monetarist experiment and the return to pre-Keynesian economic principles of 1979 to 1985 has been an undoubted and unfortunate failure; furthermore one finds it hard to escape the conclusion that in many ways the Thatcher government did not really know what it was doing, at any rate for its first two years in office. In the first place there is good reason to cast doubt on many of the fundamental theoretical premises upon which it based its policies. For example, the relationship between the money supply and inflation does not appear as straightforward as it would have had us believe, nor is that between the PSBR and monetary growth. There is also firm evidence from the United States and from the UK recession of 1980 and 1981 that fiscal policy is by no means as impotent as Friedman and his disciples suppose. Secondly, the government has found itself unable to control its chosen definitions of the money supply, which initially at least formed the centrepiece of its policy. Thirdly, in its first year in office it actually boosted inflation and sharpened inflationary expectations rather than dampening them as it intended. This made its task thereafter considerably harder and the transitional cost of its over-zealous fiscal and monetary squeeze more expensive in terms of output and jobs. Between 1980 and 1983 the total assets and capacity of manufacturing industry fell by some 24 per cent,[8] while unemployment doubled. Today (1985) unemployment is still on an upward trend and 1.21 million people have been out of work for more than a year. Such mass idleness has already created a divided society in which whole communities and areas of our inner cities have been rendered industrial and social wastelands. Hundreds of thousands of people are now to all intents and purposes unemployable and without hope. The resentment and civil unrest of recent years is inextricably bound up with unemployment and declining social conditions and cannot be ignored. There is a serious danger of a growth of political extremism and increasing violence unless people are offered more of a chance to re-establish their self-respect.

There is evidence now, in November 1985, that the government is changing course to some extent. Chancellor Lawson has been prepared to admit that the predictive power of the money supply statistics is limited, he has specifically endorsed judgement and discretion in the formulation of monetary policy, and the fiscal stance has been slightly relaxed through the rather dubious mechanism of increased asset sales. However, this latter modification in policy seems likely to offer little solace to the army of unemployed and can be seen more as a means to boost the real incomes of the employed in the run-up to the next election.

III
Is there an Alternative to Thatcherism?

The inevitable question arises, what is the alternative to Thatcherism? One thing is for certain, and that is that anybody who professes to have a simple answer to our economic problems is deluding themselves. Our difficulties are complex, often with their roots in historical and institutional factors, and will take a considerable amount of time to reverse in any real sense. Constraints impose upon potential alternative policy regimes from all sides. In addition to the inflationary bias of the labour market, any plan for increased employment must come to terms with the gradual decline in North Sea oil output, Britain's high propensity to import, the perceptions of financial markets, the temptations inherent in a parliamentary democracy, and the spread of capital, as opposed to labour, intensive technology. However, such complications are no excuse for inaction. To do nothing is the most crass of abrogations of responsibility on the part of a government. Politics is, to use R. A. Butler's term, 'the Art of the Possible'.

So where should this government, or any alternative government, start? A first step would be to explore the possibilities of greater international co-operation and co-ordination of economic policies. France's recent efforts to isolate itself from world economic trends amply illustrate the difficulties of expansion in one country. There is then the need to make the MTFS more flexible and conditional, and to rely more on Money GDP rather than some definition of money supply as the central target. The objective would be to keep the MTFS as a symbol of the government's commitment to overall fiscal and monetary continence and co-ordination, but to offer more room for manoeuvre in response to external shocks or unexpected internal developments. All economies have been subject to fluctuations for thousands of years and therefore the British economy is not likely to stop exhibiting cyclical behaviour now. Moreover, some of the downswings of these cycles are likely to be deep and protracted and there should be scope within an MTFS to allow sensible and moderate action to offset them. Financial markets must be appeased while the depression psychosis afflicting British industry must be removed. For thirty years after the war the government could be depended on to act to counter any depression and business could be confident that no downturn would last long. Thus, despite the uncertainties of 'stop–go', the Keynesian era had a strong positive underlying psychological effect on the investment and employment policies of industry which, as much as demand management itself, helped to maintain full employment. Under the present economic regime this has not been present and business confidence is by all accounts in a lamentable state.

The government should make clear its readiness to loosen fiscal policy in anticipation of the next recession likely to hit Britain. At present fiscal policy is much too bold as far as the paying off of debt is concerned. The PSBR could be allowed to expand to some 4.5 per cent of GDP (£15 billion) without increasing the burden of debt (debt:GDP ratio), which is at present close to the OECD average.[9] Financial markets could therefore, be persuaded to acquiesce in this without forcing up interest rates. There is, of course, a considerable case for increasing expenditure on Britain's inadequate and rapidly deteriorating capital infrastructure and this should be the first priority in any government-financed expansion. It would, in addition, have a more direct and extensive effect in creating jobs than tax cuts, which, given Britain's predilection for imports, would most probably create more jobs abroad than in the UK.

As far as microeconomic policy is concerned, one is forced to the conclusion that unemployment is only really likely to be reduced to anything resembling what it was in, say, 1977 or 1978 if there is a workable incomes policy. This is not to deny that the trade union reforms of 1980, 1982 and 1984 should be perservered with. No good would be served by their reversal, and their beneficial effects on wage bargaining have probably not fully worked through yet. It is, however, doubtful whether, apart from incentives to expand the number of profit-sharing schemes, any further measures to free the labour market would be worth the political difficulties they would throw up. Certainly more attacks on the low paid would be unfair and misdirected. The problem is then to devise a workable incomes policy which affects all groups of workers. As the history of the last forty years shows, this is not easy. It is a subject we shall turn to in the final chapter.

10

Conclusions

We have in the previous eight chapters traced the story of the wages problem in employment policy in the United Kingdom over the years 1936–85. In so doing we have detailed the rise and fall of Keynesian economics and of incomes policy as a means to restrain inflationary pressures in a Keynesian full employment policy environment. What conclusions can we draw from all this?

I
The Inflationary Process of the
Last Forty Years

Let us first look at the inflationary process which undermined the Keynesian era. The most important point to make is that the inflation of the years 1945–85 had its roots both in economic factors and in those of a more institutional, social and political nature. It involved both 'demand-pull' and 'cost-push' elements. On the one hand there was a tendency for successive governments to overstimulate the economy and pump too much demand into it. Wage rises in the industries most responsive to demand pressure were then transmitted to other industries as workers sought to maintain established relativities. The overstimulation of demand was often the result of poor forecasting and the difficulties inherent in predicting the economic future. Anti-cyclical measures often exercised their full effects when recovery was already in full swing. In the 1950s at least, governments also had the habit of looking at an unemployment level of, say, 500,000, much of which was confined to specific regions such as the North-East, Clydeside, or South Wales, and attempting to reduce it by a general demand stimulus, thus tightening already taut labour market conditions in much of the country. A third factor in the overheating of the economy was the political pressure acting on governments in a democratic environment where very full employment had become the norm. There was a constant temptation to keep the economy working at full capacity in the run-up to an election and to reap the vote-winning benefits this would bestow, while pooh-poohing the potential costs in terms of inflation and balance of payments difficulties which would manifest themselves later. Moreover, subsequently it became increasingly difficult fully to reverse the expansionary measures taken. As Lord Roberthall has put it, 'in a contraction the Chancellor of the Exchequer tended to be a lonely figure, while in an expansion all his colleagues were only too anxious to help'.[1]

The inflationary impetus of often excessive demand interacted with a number of other inflationary forces of a social and institutional nature which manifested themselves in the postwar era of full employment, economic growth and rapidly rising living standards, and which became increasingly strong from the late 1960s (thus undermining any precise relationship between the rate of wage inflation and the level of unemployment). These included a general intensification of the struggle for a high relative wage as individual groups came to realize more and more the power they possessed and as legislation was passed which strengthened the monopolistic position of the trade unions; the tendency of increased affluence to raise expectations and the demand for income growth continuity; a reaction against rising and more widespread taxation; and, most importantly, a growing inflation-consciousness amongst workers in the wake of a protracted period of rising prices.

Although a major cause of concern, the inflationary problem did not get seriously out of hand until fixed exchange rates were abandoned in 1972. Prior to this date inflationary pressures tended to manifest themselves quickly in the form of payments deficits, which, if a politically damaging devaluation was to be avoided, demanded a degree of retrenchment. British inflation in the 1950s and 1960s was little worse than average. After 1972, however, when the discipline imposed by the need to defend a fixed rate was no longer present, Britain's absolute and relative performance in terms of price stability was appalling, as Table 10.1 illustrates.

In 1972–3 the economy was rapidly reflated and on top of this a series of price shocks in the form of a commodity price boom and the first oil crisis hit Britain in the context of a depreciating exchange rate. Workers attempted to defend their real incomes against the impover-

Table 10.1 *Average Percentage Increase in Cost of Living in Various Countries 1950–83*

	1950–60	1960–70	1970–80	1980–83
Belgium	2.0	3.0	6.8	6.8
Denmark	3.0	5.5	9.8	10.3
France	5.7	3.6	9.6	12.2
W. Germany	1.9	2.6	5.1	4.9
Italy	3.0	3.9	14.1	17.9
Japan	4.0	5.7	9.0	4.4
Netherlands	3.1	4.1	7.0	5.5
Norway	4.5	4.5	8.6	11.6
Sweden	4.6	4.0	9.1	10.9
Switzerland	1.4	3.3	4.9	4.8
UK	4.1	4.0	13.7	10.8
USA	2.1	2.6	7.8	8.3
Average	3.3	3.9	8.8	9.0

Source: IMF, *International Financial Statistics* (New York: IMF, yearly).

ishing effects of these extraneous forces by seeking compensatory rises in wages and salaries, while the government's monetary and fiscal stance remained far too expansive and accommodatory for too long. The result was inflation rates unheard of in Britain since the post-First World War boom, and a strong reaction against Keynesian policies leading eventually to the Thatcherite Revolution of recent years.

II
Judgement on Policy-Makers early in the Keynesian Era

The second point to make is that contrary to what Balogh and Lerner said about attitudes to the wages problem amongst policy-makers early in the Keynesian era,[2] officials and economists in Whitehall were on the whole certainly neither 'innocent' nor 'dismissive' of this difficulty. Over the years 1936–51 there was an increasing realization of, and concentration on, the wages problem, which in the eyes of 'insiders' to a large degree superseded doubts about the efficacy of fiscal policy and the multiplier theory, as the major stumbling block in the implementation of Keynesian policies. In general the basic mechanics of the wage problem as it developed over the postwar period were understood at an early stage. 'Insiders' saw that employers would be more willing to grant wage increases in prosperous periods when profits were high and when they were competing for scarce labour, and that there would be an intensification of the struggle for a high relative wage at high levels of employment, manifesting itself in 'leapfrogging' behaviour. They also surmised that there would be violent reactions against large and sudden cuts in real wages.[3]

At the same time, however, it would be wrong to suggest that the extent and duration of the difficulties in the wages sphere over the following years were by any means foreseen *in toto*. For example, no economist in Whitehall during the early phases of the Keynesian era predicted that inflation-consciousness of such a highly sensitive nature would become operative and that money-illusion would by 1975 be to all intents and purposes punctured as people's expectations of inflation increasingly rapidly matched actual inflation in a highly inflationary environment. Likewise not enough account was taken of the vulnerability of macroeconomic policy to electoral opportunism. While some Treasury officials such as Sir Frederick Phillips sought to hang on to the balanced budget rule of thumb of the 1930s for just this reason, the economists simply did not think it credible that politicians would pursue the feckless expansion of budget deficits and the issue of pound notes to gain votes. Their implicit assumption was the naive one that economic policy would be guided by impartial economic technocrats and could remain relatively free from political considerations. A further omission on the part of 'insiders' was their failure to predict the growth in workplace bargaining and the decentralization of wage negotiations under conditions of full employment.

But could one realistically expect a universal and comprehensive understanding of the political, social, external and institutional complexities which were brought to bear on the formulation and implementation of macroeconomic policy over the postwar era and which were at the heart of the inflation of the 1970s? The answer is obviously 'No'. Correspondingly, one must conclude that policy-makers early in the Keynesian era did an acceptable job in warning future governments about the inflationary pitfalls of Keynesian economics, and in drawing up guidelines for the new approach's effectuation. A large proportion of the blame for the economic predicaments of more recent years and the fall from grace of Keynesian economics must therefore necessarily lie with the latter-day politicians and policy-makers, who forgot much of the advice put forward early in the Keynesian era. Certainly a less expansive, more consistent and less accommodatory money-demand management policy as originally specified in the 1944 White Paper would, had it proved possible to introduce it from the outset, have made it easier to avoid accelerating inflation. The damaging political trade cycle which helped to lock in successfully higher rates of inflation and inflationary expectations would also have been avoided, and pure Keynesian policies might still be an option available in a real depression. Admittedly under such a regime the ultra high levels of employment of the 1950s and 1960s might not have been realized, but the growth and dynamism of the world economy was such over this period that until the collapse of the Bretton Woods-IMF fixed exchange rate system and the first OPEC price shock, an individual economy as open as Britain's would most probably have experienced historically high levels of employment in any case.

What is also obvious is that as far as more direct potential solutions to the wages problem in a full employment environment are concerned, most of the forms of incomes policy resorted to over the more recent postwar years were discussed in Whitehall at least in outline in the period 1941–51. This was a time when it was impracticable to limit the commitment to full employment because of the circumstances of war, reconstruction and rearmament, and when many 'insiders' thought that even if a more conservative approach to demand management were adopted, some form of wage restraint or a modified approach to collective bargaining would be needed in any case to ensure an acceptable division between jobs and prices. In studying the incomes policies introduced thereafter, one is constantly struck by a sense of *déjà vu*. Everything from statutory fixed wage norms to outside advisory bodies on wages and inflation taxes was propounded by 'insiders' at an early stage in the Keynesian era.

III
The Nature of Postwar Incomes Policies

Although the first, and arguably the most successful, incomes policy introduced over the postwar era ran from 1948 to 1950, incomes policy's golden age in Britain was in the years 1961–79. In the 1950s, despite the urgings of the Chief Economic Adviser and the fact that the subject was frequently on the Cabinet's agenda, there was a reluctance to intervene directly in the labour market and a preference for varying degrees of reasoned persuasion in regard to wages. It was easy to acquiesce in this while relatively depressed commodity prices helped to keep the domestic price index down. Thereafter incomes policies became very much the rule rather than the exception, although they varied widely in format. We have seen statutory policies as in 1972–4, voluntary policies as in 1974–5, policies applying predominantly to the public sector as in 1970–71 and freezes as in 1966. We have seen policies designed to be long-term or reformist, and policies designed to be short- or medium-term. We have also seen efforts to reduce inflationary pressure by attacking the monopoly power of trade unions. Most often there has been a 'norm' or guideline for pay settlements designed to bring about price stability, or a drastic reduction in the rate of inflation. These have been expressed both in terms of a percentage figure, and of a flat-rate increase. The norms, which unfortunately came to be regarded as minima rather than average figures, have tended to be policed to some extent by a form of outside body sponsored by the government, such as the National Board on Prices and Incomes, or the Pay Board. The norms have also been coupled with a list of acceptable reasons for an increase and of cases where exceptions to the general rule were permitted, the latter being designed to provide the policy with some kind of flexibility. The most common exceptions granted have been to improve the living standards of those on very low incomes, to allow for the reallocation of labour, or where higher pay settlements could be financed by productivity improvements. At the same time most incomes policies have sought explicitly to deter 'comparability claims' and the linking of pay rises to the cost of living. Stage III of Mr Heath's incomes policy was, of course, an unfortunate exception as far as indexation was concerned. Incomes policies have tended to be coupled in varying degrees with efforts to obtain some form of consensus of support by offering concessions to wage earners in other areas of economic and social policy. Thus governments implementing incomes policies have become involved to varying degrees in macroeconomic bargaining with trade union and employer representatives, discussing with them matters ranging from growth targets to pensions, dividends and prices in an effort to assemble a package acceptable to the leaders of both sides of industry. Such developments have thrown up issues all of their own, including questions of infringement of parliamentary democracy.

IV
The Failure of Postwar
Incomes Policies

Allowing for the difficulties in isolating the effects of incomes policies from other forces impinging upon the movement of wages and prices, such as unemployment and exchange rate variations, and the fact that sometimes, as in 1963–4 or 1969–71, it is hard to say whether an incomes policy was in operation, one cannot but conclude that incomes policies have repeatedly failed to live up to expectations. A period of about two years has seemed to be the maximum length of time over which it can be claimed that any policy has held. Thereafter there has tended to be a backlash against restraint and a period of industrial strife in which pay settlements compensating for the years of forebearance have been obtained. This in turn has been frequently followed by the fall of the government. The most successful form of incomes policy has tended to be the temporary freeze imposed in a crisis, and whereby all wage earners could be reasonably sure that for a time at least they were being treated alike. Patience with such policies has soon run out, however, as anomalies have begun to mount up (no freeze could ever be 100 per cent effective), and workers to become increasingly conscious that their living standards were suffering. But it proved even more difficult to graduate from the simple, rigid formula of a freeze to something more flexible and lasting. Public sympathy for incomes policy has tended to wane all too rapidly, while the political will of governments to carry through an incomes policy has evaporated at about the same rate.

In analysing the underlying reasons for the failure of incomes policies, one can discern a number of important factors. In the first place incomes policies have frequently been asked to do far too much, bearing in mind the demand conditions. To take 1964–7 and 1972–4 as examples, in both these periods incomes policy was to a large degree undermined by overexpansionary demand management policies which accelerated wage drift. Despite what may have been fixed as the norm for wages at a national level, as activity boomed on the shop floor, shop stewards, rate fixers and individual workers found themselves in such a strong bargaining position that they exerted continued upward pressure on piece rates and local supplementary payments. Employers, anxious not to lose either production or manpower, acquiesced in these demands. Thus the national norm was breached and tension grew between those able to gain from wage drift and those who could not. Strong forces were set in motion to re-establish disturbed relativities and differentials, and the incomes policy was further undermined. British governments took a long time to understand the nature and extent of this process, and it is an extremely difficult process to arrest completely in a free democratic society. However, better tailored demand management policies would have helped to reduce its potency and given incomes policy a better chance of success.

A second and not unrelated matter which tended to denude the effectiveness of British incomes policies over the postwar era was the institutional framework within which they were asked to operate. British employers have always by international standards been weak in a collective sense. Possible explanations for this include Britain's early industrialization and technological lead, which tended to limit price competition, and the development of a non-Marxist trade union movement. But whatever the exact causes, British employers have never developed strong industry-wide coalitions and have always valued their independence extremely highly. The full employment and decentralization of the wage bargaining process of the initial postwar years has exacerbated this tendency. While in recent years the CBI has been active in building up its co-ordinating role by introducing an annual conference, developing more extensive regional organization and setting up local pay conferences and a small 'President's Committee' to formulate and run policy, it has tended on the whole to be an unwieldy, conservative body unable and unwilling to exert any great central co-ordination over its members. As employers grant pay increases, if an incomes policy is to hold, it requires a strong and consistent stance from them. This has never in truth been present.

The centrifugal forces operative amongst employers in Britain have also come to have major repercussions on the trade union movement. A splintered TUC, made up of an enormous number of individual unions organized on an occupational basis, and with an increasingly maverick shop floor, has been given no concerted and long-term incentive by employers in the form of a tough bargaining posture, to restructure, reorganize and increase co-ordination. It is noticeable that it is only when it is under attack, as at the time of the publication of the White Paper *In Place of Strife*, or the Industrial Relations Act, that the TUC increases its co-ordinating activities via multi-union campaigns, more regional organization, and so on. The movement to decentralization in wage bargaining of the postwar years was allowed to go on largely unchecked and the chances of any centrally imposed incomes policy working were reduced because the two major institutions, the TUC and the CBI, were ill-equipped to stop it.

A third factor in the failure of incomes policies over the postwar era is the question of how much an incomes policy is ever in the self-interest of the trade unions. Some politicians and economists have stated during the period under consideration that the failure of the trade union movement to support incomes policy is absurd and stupid, and certainly a strong case can be made for this point of view. For example, the limitation of wage increases to the average rate of growth of productivity in the economy should in theory preserve the underlying rate of increase in real incomes, while arresting inflation more or less completely. Furthermore, by assuring employers of stable wage costs, wage restraint might well increase the propensity to invest and the actual growth rate. It would also ensure that British goods were kept competitive in world markets and that the external account was kept in balance. However, a detailed inspection of the implications of wage restraint both for workers and trade unions as institutions suggests that there are very potent and logical reasons why union leaders and individuals have tended to dislike such policies.

In the first place, a simplistic policy, such as a freeze, or the limitation of wage increases to a uniform figure, has tended to deprive union negotiators of undertaking what they see as their most important role: the negotiation of wage increases with employers. Furthermore, the more complex policies have tended to involve review processes utilizing government-sponsored boards or TUC committees. These processes often resulted in delays or disappointing outcomes, which only served to enhance the desire of union negotiators for freedom of action in their trade. If a union cannot take action to try to meet its members' wishes, those members might mount an unofficial strike, or attempt to install a new union leadership which would more actively follow their wishes. The objectives of price stability and the maintenance of high employment are naturally important to trade union negotiators, but not so important as the maintenance of trade union integrity and bargaining strength, and the preservation of the leaders' position and power.

Merely because large money-wage increases might have inflationary repercussions, does not necessarily mean that unions or individual workers will be willing to forego them. Such increases might, in historical perspective or by the standards of the contemporary wage

141

round, be above average and thus help to draw new members into the union and to cement the position of the leader. It can be especially important for new union leaders, seeking to prove their worth, to achieve high money-wage increases. For the workers, such increases will provide reasonably certain protection against inflation and against falling back in the league table of relative wages.

Any incomes policy tends to imply some judgement about the appropriate distribution of income amongst trade unionists, as no incomes policy can be neutral with respect to relative wages. A simple across-the-board freeze will stymie those seeking to change the existing distribution of awards; a wage policy using a percentage norm will widen differentials, while a flat-rate system tends to narrow differentials. All add up to resentment from some quarter and all are likely to lead to intra-union squabbles which show up the TUC in a bad light.

Wage restraint requires the trade union movement to abandon the 'class struggle' at an industrial level. Restraint, especially that designed to be long-term or permanent, effectively implies that the union movement has rejected the notion of using aggressive wage bargaining to alter radically the distribution of income. Even the most moderate union leaders might well be highly reluctant to pass up this right, which for long has lain at the very heart of trade union ideology.

Finally, wage restraint is subject to the paradox of collective action. By this I mean that although collective action might well be very much in the self-interest of a group, that action will not survive over a protracted period of time if its benefits are bestowed indiscriminately upon those who take part and those who do not. This is because constituent parts of the group will maximize their utility if they refuse to undertake the action, as they will still reap its benefits without having to pay any of its costs. Naturally enough, if all the constituent units refuse to undertake the action, then there will be no benefits at all. But each individual unit, if it is small in comparison to the rest of the group, may well assume that its own contribution to the achievement of the desired result is so small as not to be missed. Thus individual unions, even after the union movement as a whole might have agreed to a policy of wage restraint, might well perceive it as possible to obtain large wage increases without jeopardizing the desired result of a reduction in wage inflation. Of course, the more unions who think this way, the more likely that general acquiescence will break down and the policy fall flat.

Another reason behind the failure of postwar incomes policies is the

fact that it has generally proved much easier to police wage negotiations in the public sector than the private sector. This has rapidly
created tensions and the demand for the re-establishment of relativities. The tendency of governments to set norms too low in comparison
to the current rate of inflation or the going rate of wage increases has
also led to the decay of wage restraint all too soon. Moreover,
governments have consistently failed to present incomes policies to the
public in a suitably coherent and intelligible way over a protracted
period. To change the bargaining habits of decades takes much more
than a press conference at the time a White Paper is published. Finally,
other policies in regard to the exchange rate or taxation, both direct
and indirect, have often proved incompatible with the success of a wage
policy.

V
Incomes Policy: the Future

Despite the undoubted failure of incomes policy over the postwar era,
at the end of the last chapter I made clear my belief that if unemployment was to be reduced without a resurgence in inflation, an incomes
policy, coupled with a more flexible, though still essentially continent,
financial policy, was the best means to that end. Thus, despite
spending much of the book detailing the failures of Keynesian policy-
making, I am proposing what has been called 'restructured' or 'new'
Keynesianism to alleviate the economic problems of today. To me, a
Keynesian approach modified to incorporate the lessons of the last fifty
years offers us all, and the unemployment in particular, a lot more hope
in the long term than the monetarism of recent years. I have already
outlined my suggestions for demand management policy and on union
legislation, it is now the turn of wages policy. What form of wages
policy would in future offer the best hope of providing more jobs and
less inflation?

The first point to make in regard to any future incomes policy is that
it should have long-term aims, and that people should not expect it to
enjoy instant success. Its acceptance and efficacy will, however, be
hastened by the government's making strenuous and consistent efforts
to persuade public opinion that it is both necessary and fair in the
circumstances. This is likely to involve an extensive process of
explanation, debate and education in a form that is intelligible to the

man in the street. It will require patience and no little skill in the art of public relations. But recent years have seen governments and political parties making increasingly effective use of media campaigns, so the biggest obstacle to the implementation of such an effort will most likely prove to be a lack of political will.

Obviously the chances of the policy succeeding will be greatly increased if it can command the active support of both sides of industry, and the TUC and CBI in particular. There will be a need for regular tripartite discussion on the scope for wage increases in the economy. The government could, for example, each year, towards the end of the current wage round, present to the employers and unions a series of scenarios incorporating the potential effects on the economy over the next twelve months of differing levels of pay settlements in the context of the MTFS, in the hope that agreement could be reached on what was the 'right level'. What is certain is that there is a need to seek some form of consensus on wage bargaining behaviour.

Let us now suppose that after a series of tripartite meetings, the government announces that over the next wage round the average settlement should be x per cent. The government cannot then afford to rely merely on the good intentions of the employers to hold wages to this level and a promise (which in any case may not be forthcoming) from the unions to exercise self-restraint. To hold pay settlements close to that norm it is likely that sanctions will be required, and it appears to me that the most effective would be tax disincentives on employers. Inflationary rises in the total earnings bill for a company above the level emerging from the national discussions should be made the subject of tax payments. Such an approach would make allowance for the present decentralized nature of the bargaining process. It would also, by improving the co-ordination of employer resistance to wage claims, actually help to reduce the decentralized nature of collective bargaining and still allow the trade unions scope to bargain. There would be no compulsion as such involved. The policy would merely seek to change decisions without changing the basic format (collective bargaining) within which decisions are reached. A firm can make any decision it is disposed to do as long as it is prepared to pay the consequences. Finally it would be flexible in that it would allow management some leeway in paying more to attract certain skills without being penalized. [4]

Obviously this tax-based incomes policy would not be perfect, and would give rise to a number of problems. For a start the British Inland Revenue has never before been involved in the running of incomes policy, and it would be bound to take time in adapting to its new role. The policy could not possibly be extended to all companies. This would be administratively out of the question. It would most likely have to be limited to companies in the private sector employing more than 1,000 workers. Thus, under 20,000 companies would be involved in comparison to nearly a million pay points for PAYE. The system, by being limited to large firms, would leave the danger that some parts of the economy likely to offer the biggest threat to an incomes policy would have to be excluded from its direct effects. Small firms in construction or road haulage, for example, might become 'wage leaders' by securing settlements above the norm and trigger pressures in those areas covered by the policy. There is a danger, therefore, that an inflation-tax-based incomes policy might decay like any other incomes policy. There would also be the danger of oligopolies, with their strong market position, passing the tax on in price increases. As for dealing with the public sector it has been suggested that the best solution to the enormous potential problems in this area would be the application of the norm for government employees together with a formula for evening up with the private sector, all backed up by cash limits on public expenditure. It is probable, however, that such a policy would have to be operated by a special body for the public sector.

The difficulties involved in running this type of incomes policy, or indeed any incomes policy, would be greatly reduced by a movement towards a common pay settlement date, at least as far as major pay negotiations are concerned, as this would help to lessen the threat of claims building on each other as the pay round develops. This would not be easy to achieve, but it has been discussed by government, unions and employers before and it might therefore be put forward at an early stage in the above-mentioned tripartite discussions. Perhaps the limited goal of a progression from private sector deals in the autumn through to public sector deals in the spring and the run-up to the budget could be achieved within a few years.

An inflation tax system of wage restraint is never going to prove to be a political tea-party, and no doubt will throw up a good number of unforeseen problems and complexities. It will require a lot of ministerial stamina to see it through. However, if coupled with a sensible financial policy, it does seem to me to offer more hope to the unemployed and more of a potential solution to the wage problem than either more traditional incomes policies or monetarism. As Maurice Chevalier said of old age: 'It is better than the alternative.'

Notes

Chapter 1: Introduction

1 Cmd 6527 (1944).
2 HM Treasury, 'Memorandum on monetary policy', in Treasury and Civil Service Committee, *Monetary Policy*, Vol. II. HC 164-II (London: HMSO, 1981).
3 See comments by Alan Budd on Sir Bryan Hopkin, 'The development of demand management', in F. Cairncross (ed.), *Changing Perceptions of Economic Policy* (London: Methuen, 1981), p. 52.
4 T. Balogh, *The Irrelevance of Conventional Economics* (London: Weidenfeld & Nicolson, 1981), pp. 47–8.
5 A. P. Lerner, 'Employment theory and employment policy', *American Economic Review*, Vol. lvii, March 1967, p. 1.

Chapter 2: The General Theory, the Treasury and the Wages Problem 1936–9

1 C. H. Feinstein, *National Income, Expenditure and Output of the United Kingdom, 1855–1965* (Cambridge: Cambridge University Press, 1972), Table 57, pp. 125–7. S. Howson, 'Slump and unemployment', in R. Floud and D. McCloskey (eds), *The Economic History of Britain since 1700, Part II* (Cambridge: Cambridge University Press, 1981), p. 265.
2 By which Keynes referred not only to what we now, after Marx, call the 'Classical' economists, such as Smith, Ricardo and Mill, but also to what we now refer to as the 'neo-Classical' school, including such eminent names as Marshall and Edgeworth. All references to 'Classical' economists in this book should be interpreted as consistent with Keynes's definition of the term.
3 This was despite some concessions to increased government intervention in the form of the management of sterling, protection and Imperial Preference, and Special Areas Policy.
4 In the introduction to *The General Theory* Keynes stated his aim 'of persuading economists to re-examine certain of their basic assumptions ... to bring to an issue the deep divergencies of opinion between fellow economists which have for the time being almost destroyed the practical influence of economic theory'. J. M. Keynes, *The Collected Writings of John Maynard Keynes* (hereafter cited as *J.M.K.*), Vol. vii, *The General Theory of Employment, Interest and Money* (London: Macmillan, 1973), p. xi.
5 ibid., p. 5.

6 Preference for increases in government expenditure was derived from the following factors:

(1) Government expenditure is exhaustive on the first round and so 'multiplier' effects are more potent than for a given change in taxation.
(2) Keynes's diagnosis of underemployment equilibrium centred on a deficiency in investment and, as such, the optimum remedy was one which acted on investment directly.
(3) No machinery or legal powers then existed to permit regulation of taxes outside budgets.

7 James Meade's essay 'The Keynesian Revolution', in M. Keynes (ed.), *Essays on John Maynard Keynes* (London: Cambridge University Press, 1975), p. 82, provides the best description of these vital elements in the 'Keynesian' schema. For a critique of Keynes's approach, see W. Eltis, 'The failure of the Keynesian conventional wisdom', *Lloyds Bank Review*, n.s. no. 122, October 1976, p. 1.

8 Keynes, *J.M.K.*, Vol. vii, p. 10.

9 ibid., p. 14.

10 W. Leontieff, 'The fundamental assumption of Mr. Keynes' Monetary Theory of Employment', *Quarterly Journal of Economics*, Vol. li, November 1936, p. 192.

11 I. Fisher, *The Money Illusion* (New York: St Martin's Press, 1928), p. 61.

12 Keynes, *J.M.K.*, Vol. vii, chapter on 'The theory of prices', p. 292.

13 Lord Kahn, 'On re-reading Keynes', *Proceedings of the British Academy*, Vol. lx, 1974, p. 371, hereafter cited as 'Re-reading Keynes', and 'On the development of Keynes' thought', *Journal of Economic Literature*, Vol. xvi, June 1978, p. 545.

The Cambridge 'circus' included Kahn, Pierro Sraffa, Joan and Austin Robinson and James Meade, with Kahn forming the channel of communication between Keynes and his 'disciples'. For further information on the 'circus' see D. Patinkin, 'The process of writing *The General Theory*', in D. Patinkin and J. C. Leith (eds), *Keynes, Cambridge and The General Theory* (London: Macmillan, 1977), p. 3.

14 See, for example, Sir J. R. Hicks, *The Crisis in Keynesian Economics* (Oxford: Blackwell, 1974), p. 59; and R. F. Harrod, 'Retrospect on Keynes', in R. Lekachman (ed.), *Keynes' General Theory: Reports of Three Decades* (New York: St Martin's Press, 1964), p. 139.

15 If Keynes had been consistent we should have expected him to have anticipated Duesenberry's analysis of consumption and saving by some thirteen years. See Keynes, *J.M.K.*, Vol. vii, p. 113, and J. S. Duesenberry, *Income, Saving and the Theory of Consumer Behaviour* (Cambridge, Mass.: Harvard University Press, 1949).

16 Kahn, 'Re-reading Keynes', p. 371.

17 J. M. Keynes, 'Borrowing for defence: is it inflation?', *The Times*, 11 March 1937.

18 See Keynes, *J.M.K.*, Vol. xxix, *The General Theory and After: A Supplement*, letter from Keynes to J. T. Dunlop, 9 April 1938, p. 284.

19 J. M. Keynes, 'The relative movements of real wages and output', *Economic Journal*, Vol. liv, March 1939, footnote on p. 40.

20 See D. E. Moggridge, *Keynes* (London: Fontana, 1976), chapters 1 and 2.

21 The Economic Advisory Council Committee on Economic Information was the weaker concomitant of the first attempt to recruit economists into government on a full-time basis, the Economic Advisory Council proper, which, after a lifespan of just over a year, fell into disuse at the time of the 1931 financial crisis. The committee consisted of several academic economists, among them Keynes and Henderson, together with more institutional figures such as Sir Josiah Stamp and Treasury officials Sir Frederick Phillips and Sir Frederick Leith-Ross. It furnished the Treasury with detailed studies of the prevailing economic environment and policy-prescriptions throughout the 1930s. The more orthodox economists on the committee joined with Keynes in recommending bolder economic policies because, though not 'Keynesian', their models of the economy allowed for the real world existence of 'special cases', likely to render the system incapable of automatically reaching full employment equilibrium. See S. Howson and D. Winch, *The Economic Advisory Council 1930–39: A Study in Economic Advice during Depression and Recovery* (Cambridge: Cambridge University Press, 1977).

22 See G. C. Peden, 'Keynes, the Treasury and unemployment in the later nineteen-thirties', *Oxford Economic Papers*, n.s., Vol. xxxii, March 1980, p. 1, hereafter cited as 'Keynes, the Treasury and unemployment'; and 'Sir Richard Hopkins and the "Keynesian Revolution" in employment policy 1929–45', *Economic History Review*, 2nd series, Vol. xxxvi (1983), p. 281. See also Public Record Office (London), Cabinet Office Papers, series 124, file 215A: Eady to Brook, 26 April 1944; in this note Eady states that Keynes believed the use of national income techniques to be one of the most important elements in the Keynesian Revolution and that he would have begun any White Paper on postwar employment policy with a reference to the wartime National Income and Expenditure White Papers. Hereafter, all Public Record Office references will be cited in the form PRO CAB 124/215A.

23 R. Middleton, 'The Treasury in the nineteen-thirties: political and administrative constraints to the acceptance of the "new" economics', *Oxford Economic Papers*, Vol. xxxiv, March 1982, p. 48 (hereafter cited as 'The Treasury in the 1930s); and A. Marwick, 'Middle opinion in the nineteen-thirties: planning, progress and political agreement', *English Historical Review*, Vol. lxxix, April 1964, p. 258.

24 Middleton, 'The Treasury in the 1930s', p. 48.

25 ibid. The elements included in both sides of government accounts varied considerable from year to year. In addition, expenditure financed by borrowing under certain Acts of Parliament was omitted, and debt redemption was included in general expenditure. On the revenue side, non-recurrent receipts, or 'raids' on extra budgetary funds, were utilized.

26 PRO T 175/17 (Pt II): Phillips to Hopkins, 28 February 1933.

27 Middleton, 'The Treasury in the 1930s', p. 48.
28 See J. Robinson, 'Full employment', in her *Collected Economic Papers*
    (Oxford: Oxford University Press, p. 176; J. R. Hicks, *Value and Capital*
    (Oxford: Clarendon, 1939), Chapter 210; J. E. Meade, *An Introduction to
    Economic Analysis and Policy* (Oxford: Clarendon, 1936), Part 1, Chap-
    ters VII and VIII; D. G. Champernowne, 'Unemployment, basic and
    monetary: the Classical analysis and the Keynesian', *Review of Economic
    Studies*, Vol. ix, June 1936, p. 202; F. A. von Hayek, *Monetary Nation-
    alism and International Stability* (Geneva: 1937), pp. 52–3; and Nuffield
    College, Oxford, Henderson Papers, file 10, 'Papers on Keynes'. My own
    M.Sc. thesis, 'The wages problem in employment policy 1936–48',
    University of Bristol, 1983, contains an analysis of all these works.
29 PRO T 208/195: R. G. Hawtrey, 'Mr. Keynes' General Theory of
    Employment, Interest and Money'.
30 PRO T 175/94 (Pt II): Hopkins to Chancellor/Sir Warren Fisher, 22
    October 1937.
31 G. C. Peden, *British Rearmament and the Treasury, 1932–39* (Edinburgh:
    Scottish Academic Press, 1979), chapters 1, 2, 6; and S. Howson,
    Domestic Monetary Management, 1919–1938 (Cambridge: Cambridge
    University Press, 1975), chapter 6.
32 Peden, 'Keynes, the Treasury and unemployment', p. 1. Also, R. A. C.
    Parker, 'British rearmament 1936–9: Treasury, trade unions and skilled
    labour', *English Historical Review*, Vol. xcvi, no. 379, April 1981, p. 306.
33 As quoted in Parker, ibid., p. 311.
34 PRO T 175/94 (Pt II): Hopkins memorandum, 30 January 1937.
35 PRO CAB 24/265, C.P. 339 (36): Leith-Ross memorandum.
36 See W. K. Hancock and M. M. Gowing, *The British War Economy*
    (London: HMSO, 1949), pp. 93–4.

Chapter 3: The Control of Wartime Inflation and the 1944 White Paper on Employment Policy

1 PRO T 175/117 (Pt II), 'Review of activities of the Ministerial Committee
   on Economic Policy', 23 January 1940.
2 See A. Bullock, *The Life and Times of Ernest Bevin*, Vol. 1 (London:
   Heinemann, 1960), p. 651, and W. S. Churchill, *The Second World War*,
   Vol. 1 (London: Cassell, 1948), p. 526.
3 See *The Conditions of Employment and National Arbitration Order* (SRO
   1940, no. 1305).
4 Cmd 6294 (1941).
5 See, for example, PRO T 230/110: memorandum by Minister of Labour,
   'Wages regulation in relation to the budget statement on the cost of living',
   16 May 1941; Robbins to Lord President's Committee, 3 March 1940, and
   T 230/114: Robbins and S. R. Dennison, 'The inter-relation of wages,
   prices and consumption', 25 March 1941.
6 J. M. Keynes, *The Collected Writings of John Maynard Keynes* (hereafter

cited as *J.M.K.*), Vol. xxii, *Activities 1939–45: Internal War Finance* (London: Macmillan, 1980), 'A supplementary note on the dimensions of the budget problem', 26 December 1940, p. 255.

7 Keynes, *J.M.K.*, Vol. xxii, Chapter 2, pp. 40–155.

8 The Labour Party, *The Nation's Wealth at the Nation's Service* (London: the Labour Party, 1938). Also, D. Jay, *Change and Fortune. A Political Record* (London: Hutchinson, 1980), pp. 78–82.

9 Letter to *The Times*, 1 March 1940.

10 *The Sources of War Finance, an Analysis and Estimate of the National Income and Expenditure in 1938 and 1940*, Cmd 6261 (1941).

11 M. Kalecki, 'The budget and inflation', *Bulletin of the Oxford Institute of Statistics*, Vol. xiii, April 1941, p. 112.

12 Trade union membership grew from 6.25 million in 1939 to nearly 8 million in 1945. Union leaders were increasingly drawn into the machinery of government via the National Joint Advisory Council, Regional Boards for Industry, the National Production Advisory Council and Joint Committees, covering some 3.5 million workers. (See S. Pollard, *The Development of the British Economy 1914–67* (London: Edward Arnold, 1976), p. 342; hereafter cited as *The Development of the British Economy*.

13

	Wage rates	Official cost of living	Wage earners cost of living	Weekly earnings
	Sept. 1939 = 100		*1938 = 100*	
1939	101	102	102.5	–
1940	111–12	119	120	130
1941	121–2	128	135	142
1942	130	129	143	160
1943	135–6	128	148	176
1944	142–3	130	150	181.5
1945	149–50	131	–	180.5

Sources: W. K. Hancock (ed.), *Statistical Digest of the Second World War* (London: HMSO, 1951), and Pollard, *The Development of the British Economy*, p. 343.

14 In the Second World War only 13,277 days were lost in nearly six years of conflict, in the First World War the figure was 26,799 in four years. Source: Dept of Employment and Productivity, *British Labour Statistics, Historical Abstract, 1886–1968* (London: HMSO, 1971), Table 197.

15 R. M. Titmuss, *Problems of Social Policy* (London: HMSO, 1950), p. 506.

16 L. Robbins, *Autobiography of an Economist* (London: Macmillan, 1971), Chapter ix (hereafter cited as *Autobiography*); and J. Jewkes, 'A defence of the White Paper on Employment Policy 1944', in *A Return to Free Market Economics? Critical Essays on Government Intervention* (London: Macmillan, 1978), p. 39 (hereafter cited as 'A defence of the White Paper . . . 1944'). For the early Treasury discussions see PRO T 160/1407/F.18876.

17 Meade's memorandum received a general endorsement from Keynes who was in Washington. See PRO T 247/90: Keynes to Meade, 6 August 1941.

18 PRO CAB 87/54: Meade, 'Internal measures for the prevention of general unemployment', 8 July 1941.

19 PRO T 230/14: 'Government intervention in the post-war transitional period', 27 May 1942, and 'Economic aspects of the proposed reforms of social security', 9 June 1942 (both by Meade).

20 PRO CAB 87/54: Tribe to Baster, undated, but early 1942; minutes of the 22nd meeting of the Committee on Post-War Internal Economic Problems.

21 PRO LAB 10/160: Tribe to Robbins, 27 January 1942.

22 PRO LAB 10/160: Robbins to Tribe, 4 May 1942.

23 PRO T 203/110: Keynes to Robbins, 15 December 1941 (comment on Robbins's note on 'Wages and inflation').

24 PRO T 230/34; Meade, 'Government intervention in the post-war economy', 8 April 1942.

25 PRO T 230/110: S. R. Dennison, 'Post-war wages policy', 30 April 1942; and J. M. Fleming, 'Post-war wages policy', undated, but after Dennison's note in the file. Also Keynes, *J.M.K.*, Vol. xxvii, *Activities 1940–46: Shaping the Post-War World: Employment and Commodities* (London: Macmillan, 1980), p. 208 (Keynes to Meade, 16 June 1942).

26 PRO T 230/34: Meade, 'Government intervention in the post-war economy', 8 April 1942.

27 PRO T 230/110: Dennison, 'Post-war wages policy', 30 April 1942.

28 PRO CAB 87/55: 'The post-war relation between purchasing power and consumer goods', 26 May 1942.

29 PRO CAB 87/13: 'The maintenance of employment', 18 May 1943.

30 PRO T 230/15: see index and Economic Section discussion papers for early 1943.

31 Keynes, *J.M.K.*, Vol. xxvii, p. 314.

32 PRO T 230/66: Meade, 'The prevention of mass unemployment', 15 February 1943; Fleming, 'The creation of employment', 19 February 1943. PRO CAB 87/13: 'The maintenance of employment', 18 May 1943.

33 PRO CAB 87/12: War Cabinet Committee on Post-War Reconstruction Priorities; minutes of meeting on 31 May 1943.

34 PRO CAB 87/55: IEP (42)21, L. Robbins, 'Ideas and policy', 26 May 1942, para. 23.

35 PRO CAB 87/63: EC (43)9, 18 October 1943, para. 16.

36 PRO CAB 87/7: 'Report of the Steering Committee on Post-War Employment', 11 January 1944.

37 Jewkes, 'A defence of the White Paper . . . 1944', p. 64.

38 PRO T 230/71: minutes of the Steering Committee on Post-War Employment.

39 PRO T 230/71: Robbins, 'Wages and prices', 16 December 1943. PRO CAB 87/7: 'Report of the Steering Committee on Post-War Employment', 11 January 1944.

40 ibid., para. 141.

41 ibid., para. 143.

42 ibid., paras 147–51.

43 See also PRO CAB 124/215A: Eady to Hopkins, 4 May 1944.

44 ibid., Eady to Hopkins, 24 April 1944.
45 *Employment Policy*, Cmd 6527 (1944), pp. 18–19, paras 49–54. Also, Nuffield College, Oxford, Henderson Papers, file 3, 'War Cabinet Committee on Reconstruction Priorities', H. D. Henderson, 'Employment policy and the balance of payments', 23 March 1944; and Henderson to Eady, 21 March 1944.
46 PRO CAB 124/695: 'Price control in the transition'. PRO CAB 87/5: 'Report of the Steering Committee on Post-War Employment', 11 January 1944, p. 63. *Employment Policy*, Cmd 6527 (1944), para. 53. Also interviews with Sir Alec Cairncross, Miss Nita Watts, Professor S. R. Dennison.
47 Interviews with Sir Alec Cairncross and Miss Nita Watts.
48 Robbins, *Autobiography*, p. 231.
49 PRO T 230/68: Meade to Robbins, 19 April 1944.
50 PRO T 230/66: Fleming, 'The creation of employment', 19 February 1943.
51 PRO CAB 87/19: minutes of the Reconstruction Advisory Council, 21 June 1944.
52 Congress House, TUC File T.1254: minutes of the 13th meeting of the Economic Committee, 14 June 1944, esp. item 80, 'Employment policy – Government White Paper', and the relevant memorandum, 13/1, of the same title.
53 *The Interim Report on Post-War Reconstruction* was thrashed out over the spring and summer of 1944. On economic matters the TUC used the services of three outside advisers, Joan Robinson, E. M. F. Durbin and G. D. H. Cole. See Congress House, TUC File T.1254: minutes and memoranda of the 8th–18th meetings of the Economic Committee, 1944.
54 TUC, *Interim Report on Post-War Reconstruction* (London: TUC, 1944), pp. 29f.
55 Congress House, TUC File T.1254: Economic Committee memorandum 1/8, 'Report of meeting with the President of the Board of Trade', 14 March 1945.
56 Keynes, *J.M.K.*, Vol. xxvii, Part II, pp. 203–419.
57 J. E. Meade, *Stagflation*, Vol. 1 (London: Allen & Unwin, 1982), p. 24. Meade reiterated this to the author in a letter dated 13 March 1982.
58 Keynes, *J.M.K.*, Vol. xxii, p. 228 ('Notes on the budget II, price and wage policy', 29 September 1940).
59 J. M. Keynes, 'The objective of international price stability', a rejoinder to F. A. Hayek's 'A commodity reserve currency', in *Economic Journal*, Vol. liii, June 1943, p. 185. See also Keynes, *J.M.K.*, Vol. xxvi, *Activities 1941–46: Shaping the Post-War World: Bretton Woods and Reparations* (London: Macmillan, 1980), pp. 36–8, Keynes to B. Graham, 31 December 1943, in which Keynes makes a similar statement.
60 ibid.
61 J. M. Keynes, 'A note by Lord Keynes', on an article by B. Graham, *Economic Journal*, Vol. liv, December 1944, p. 429.
62 As quoted in Lord Kahn, 'On re-reading Keynes', *Proceedings of the British Academy*, Vol. lx, 1974, p. 371, and E. A. G. Robinson, 'Keynes:

economist, author, statesman', *Proceedings of the British Academy*, Vol. lvii, 1971, p. 197.
63 Keynes, *J.M.K.*, Vol. xxvii, p. 405, Keynes to T. S. Eliot, 5 April 1945.
64 ibid., pp. 364–79.
65 Meade endorsed this in a letter to the author dated 3 March 1982.
66 For Keynes's views on inflation, see *J.M.K.*, Vol. ii, *The Economic Consequences of the Peace* (London: Macmillan, 1971), pp. 148–9, and *J.M.K.*, Vol. iv, *A Tract on Monetary Reform* (London: Macmillan, 1971), p. 36.
67 Interview with Professor S. R. Dennison. See also J. M. Keynes, 'The balance of payments of the United States', *Economic Journal*, Vol. lvi, June 1946, p. 172; C. Clark, *Taxmanship* (London: IEA, 1970); and F. A. von Hayek, *A Tiger by the Tail* (London: IEA, 1977), p. 103.

Chapter 4: Wages Policy and the Attlee Governments

1 Information from Dr Susan Howson.
2 Labour Party, *Let Us Face the Future* (1945).
3 *Employment Policy*, Cmd 6527 (1944), Foreword.
4 British Library of Political and Economic Science (hereafter cited as BLPES): diary of James Meade, 1/5, entry for 13 January 1946.
5 *Statement on the Economic Considerations Affecting Relations between Employers and Workers*, Cmd 7018 (1947), Foreword.
6 PRO CAB 124/786: G. Isaaacs to H. Morrison, 16 January 1947.
7 See, for example, PRO CAB 132/1: minutes of the Lord President's Committee, 29 March 1946; and PRO CAB 132/6: various memoranda by Shinwell.
8 PRO CAB 124/898: J. E. Meade to the Lord President, 24 January 1946. The Economic Section thought that the benefit of food subsidies in reducing the size of the wage claims was more than offset by the heavy budgetary cost, the distortion of consumption and the weakening of employer resistance they generated. It argued for a reduction of the subsidies and their replacement by child allowances and cuts in indirect taxation. In the financial year 1946–7, around £1 million a day was being spent on the subsidies; a sum which exceeded half the budget deficit. It was not until the 1949 budget that Sir Stafford Cripps imposed on subsidy expenditure a ceiling which stuck.
9 Isaacs had been President of the National Society of Operative Printers, Graphical and Media Personnel (NATSOPA) and a member of the TUC General Council.
10 Cmd 7321 (1948).
11 *Hansard*, Vol. 446, HC Deb., 5s., 6 August 1947, col. 1514.
12 PRO LAB 10/664: 'Working Party on the Stabilisation of Wages'.
13 PRO T 238/65: 'Report of Working Party on the Stabilisation of Wages', 22 September 1947.

14 PRO T 229/85: minutes and memoranda of the Official Working Party on the Stabilisation of Wages.

15 *Statement on Personal Incomes, Costs, and Prices*, Cmd 7321 (1948), para. 7(a). Towards the end of 1947 the TUC had made it clear 'that any attempt on the part of an outside body to regulate or directly control wage movements would have disastrous effects . . . if there was to be greater restraint upon wage movements it could come only from within the trade union movement itself. . .'. See TUC 'Interim Report on the Economic Situation', reprinted in TUC, *A Policy for Real Wages* (London: TUC, 1948).

16 *Statement on Personal Incomes, Costs and Prices*, Cmd 7321 (1948), para. 7.

17 TUC, *A Policy for Real Wages*. The policy was accepted by 5,420,000 votes to 2,032,000.

18 PRO CAB 128/15: 15th Cabinet Conclusions, 28 February 1949. *Hansard*, Vol. 464, HC·Deb., 5s., no. 107, cols. 645–6.

19 PRO T 229/213: 'Draft report of Working Party on Wages Policy and Devaluation', 6 August 1948.

20 PRO CAB 128/16: 64th and 66th Cabinet Conclusions, 7 November 1949 and 14 November 1949.

21 The majority was 657,000 out of a total vote of 7,899,000.

22 PRO T 171/400: 'The 1950–1951 budget', BC(50)13. My thanks also to Lord Roberthall for this information.

23 PRO T 172/2033: TUC, 'Wages policy – draft statement for circulation to affiliated unions', 19 June 1950.

24 PRO T 229/154: 'A first look at 1955' by Economic Section, Central Economic Planning Staff and Central Statistical Office, 10 March 1949. One of the conclusions of this memorandum was that 'present indications are that the economy may still be under inflationary strain even in 1955'.

25 PRO T 172/2033: 'The reason for a wages policy' by the Economic Section, 15 September 1950.

26 PRO CAB 124/1197: 'Wages policy 1948–52'.

27 ibid.: 'Wages policy' by the Chancellor of the Exchequer, 28 April 1950.

28 PRO CAB 134/224: Economic Policy Committee, 31st Conclusions, 18 December 1950.

29 PRO CAB 124/1197: 'Wages policy' by the Chancellor of the Exchequer, 28 April 1950.

30 PRO T 230/2033: 'Wages policy' by E. E. Bridges, 28 April 1950.

31 PRO T 229/323: 'Synopsis of a White Paper on full employment, prices and incomes', unsigned, undated.

32 Bevan became Minister of Labour in January 1951. He resigned in April 1951.

33 My thanks again to Lord Roberthall for this information.

34 PRO T 172/2033: 'Report by Chancellor on his discussions with TUC representatives on 6-2-1951', 7 February 1951.

35 PRO CAB 134/230: 'Economic policy' by the Chancellor of the Exchequer, 22 June 1951.

36 Information again from Lord Roberthall. See also P. M. Williams (ed.),

The Diary of Hugh Gaitskell 1945–1956 (London: Cape, 1983), entry for 10 August 1951, p. 268. Voluntary dividend restraint broke down in December 1950. The government in fact fell before this new policy became law.

37 For examples of 'insiders' perceptions of the wage-determination process see PRO CAB 134/189: 'Wages and prices policy and means of carrying out planning decisions', report by steering committee, 21 December 1946, and PRO T 229/323: 'Synopsis of a White Paper on full employment, prices and incomes', unsigned, undated.

38 For the full story of the United Nations initiative on full employment policy see PRO T 230/230.

39 PRO CAB 124/898: J. E. Meade to the Lord President, 24 December 1946.

40 This figure also shows up how demand conditions were much more conducive to the success of the 1948 wage policy than to the 1949 policy or the approach to the trade unions in February 1951.

41 G. Sayers Bain and R. Price, 'Union growth: dimensions, determinants and destiny', in G. Sayers Bain (ed.), *Industrial Relations in Britain* (Oxford: Blackwell, 1983), Table 11.

42 An additional indicator of trade union restraint in this period is provided by the number of days lost through strike action. In the year 1946–7 the average was 2.3 million per annum and in the years 1948–50 1.7 million. In the war years the average was 1.9 million and in the reconstruction period 1919–23, the figure was a remarkable 35.6 million per annum.

43 Respectively TUC General Secretary, General Secretary of the Transport and General Workers' Union (TGWU), General Secretary of the General and Municipal workers' Union (GMWU) and President of the National Union of Mineworkers (NUM).

44 In addition to the NJAC the Attlee governments sponsored quasi-corporate bodies such as the National Production Advisory Council for Industry and the Economic Planning Board.

45 Cripps was forced to retire in October 1950. Bevin had to accept demotion in March 1951, by which time he was a shadow of his former self. He died six weeks after his appointment as Lord Privy Seal.

46 K. Hawkins, *British Industrial Relations 1945–1975* (London: Barrie & Jenkins, 1976).

Chapter 5: Thirteen Years of Tory Economic Policy

1 PRO T 229/409: Hall to Bridges, 19 November 1951.
2 PRO T 229/402: Hall to Bridges, 28 November 1951.
3 ibid.
4 PRO T 230/297: R. L. Hall to E. N. Plowden, 23 January 1952 and E. N. Plowden to Chancellor, 29 January 1952.
5 PRO T 230/297: Butler to Hall, 31 January 1952.

6   See PRO T 229/405: 'Chancellor's meetings with TUC leaders'.
7   PRO T 227/261: S. C. Leslie to Sir B. Gilbert, 25 June 1954.
8   ibid: E. E. Bridges to Economic Secretary, 26 April 1954.
9   ibid: S. C. Leslie to Sir B. Gilbert, 28 June 1954.
10 ibid: 'Draft White Paper on full employment and price stability', 18 June 1954.
11 ibid: Economic Secretary to Chancellor, 5 July 1954; PRO T 230/299: R. L. Hall to Petch, 6 July 1954.
12 ibid: 'Draft White Paper on full employment and price stability', by R. Maudling, undated.
13 ibid: R. Armstrong to Sir B. Gilbert, 9 July 1954 and S. C. Leslie to E. E. Bridges, 21 July 1954.
14 Cmd 9725 (1956).
15 Information from Lord Roberthall. See also PRO T 230/300 'National Wages Policy and Full Employment Policy 1955'. The Cabinet had in fact been ready to publish this White Paper in the previous December, but the Cabinet reshuffle of that month meant its release was delayed until the spring.
16 *The Economic Implications of Full Employment*, Cmd 9725 (1956), pp. 10–11.
17 Quoted in Aubrey Jones, *The New Inflation: the Politics of Prices and Incomes* (Harmondsworth: Penguin, 1973), p. 49.
18 *Hansard*, Vol. 524, HC Deb., 5s., 25 July 1957, cols 650–51.
19 Information from Lord Roberthall.
20 ibid.
21 A. W. Phillips, 'The relationship between unemployment and the rate of change of money-wages in the United Kingdom 1861–1957', *Economica*, n.s., Vol. xxv, November 1958, p. 283.
22 *Council on Prices, Productivity and Incomes, Fourth Report* (London: HMSO, 1961), p. 24.
23 W. Fellner *et al.*, *The Problem of Rising Prices* (Paris: OEEC, 1961).
24 R. L. Hall, 'Britain's Economic problems', *The Economist*, 16 September 1961, p. 1042.
25 *Hansard*, Vol. 645, HC Deb, 5s, July 1961, cols 222–3.
26 Information from Professor Sir Alec Cairncross.
27 Cmnd 1626 (February 1962).
28 Harold MacMillan, *At the End of the Day, 1961–3* (London: Macmillan, 1973), p. 47 and pp. 84–5.
29 TUC, *Annual Report 1962* (London: TUC, 1962), pp. 369–70.
30 *Council on Prices, Productivity and Incomes, Fourth Report* (London: HMSO, 1961), p. 29.

Chapter 6: The Wilson Governments 1964–70

1   TUC, *Report of the 95th Annual Trades Union Congress at Brighton* (London: TUC, 1963), p. 409.

2 Quoted in W. H. Fishbein, *Wage Restraint by Concensus: Britain's Search For an Incomes Policy Agreement 1965–79* (London: Routledge & Kegan Paul, 1984), p. 37.
3 TUC, *Report of the 96th Annual Trades Union Congress at Blackpool* (London: TUC, 1964), p. 561.
4 Quoted in F. T. Blackaby (ed.), *British Economic Policy 1960–74, Demand Management* (Cambridge: Cambridge University Press for NIESR, 1978), p. 366.
5 The statement is reproduced in TUC, *Productivity, Prices and Incomes: Report of a Conference of Executive Committees of Affiliated Organisations held on 30th April 1965* (London: TUC, 1965).
6 *Prices and Incomes Policy*, Cmnd 2639 (1965).
7 Harold Wilson, *The Labour Government 1964–1970. A Personal Record* (London: Weidenfeld & Nicolson, 1971), pp. 131–2.
8 Cmnd 2808 (1965).
9 *Prices and Incomes Standstill*, Cmnd 3073 (1966).
10 *Prices and Incomes Policy: Period of Severe Restraint*, Cmnd 3150 (1966).
11 *Prices and Incomes Policy after 30 June 1967*, Cmnd 3235 (1967).
12 *Productivity, Prices and Incomes Policy in 1968 and 1969*, Cmnd 3590 (1968).
13 TUC, *Economic Review 1968* (London: TUC, 1968).
14 A. K. Cairncross and B. Eichengreen, *Sterling in Decline* (Oxford: Blackwell, 1983), p. 208.
15 *NBPI Report No. 65, Payment by Results Systems*, Cmnd 3627 (1968), para. 220 et seq.
16 *Royal Commission on Trade Unions and Employers Associations 1965–1968 Report*, Cmnd 3623 (1968), para. 1020.
17 *In Place of Strife: A Policy for Industrial Relations*, Cmnd 3888 (1969).
18 *Productivity, Prices and Incomes Policy After 1969*, Cmnd 4237 (1969).
19 Quoted in K. Hawkins, *British Industrial Relations 1945–75* (London: Barrie & Jenkins, 1976), p. 133.
20 Alex A. Jarrat, 'A workable incomes policy for Britain', in F. T. Blackaby (ed.), *An Incomes Policy for Britain* (London: Heinemann, 1972), p. 26.
21 H. Clegg, *How to Run an Incomes Policy and Why We Made Such a Mess of the Last One* (Oxford: Blackwell, 1971), p. 38.
22 Jarrat, op. cit., p. 26.

Chapter 7: Mr Heath, Incomes Policy and the Miners 1970–74

1 Quoted in W. Keegan and R. Penant-Rea, *Who Runs the Economy? Control and Influence in British Economic Policy* (London: Temple Smith, 1979), p. 180.
2 See Andrew Dean, 'Earnings in public and private sectors 1950–78', *National Institute of Economic and Social Research Review*, no. 74, November 1975, p. 63.

3 TUC, *Annual Report 1972* (London: TUC, 1973), p. 478.
4 Sir Leo Pliatzky, *Getting and Spending. Public Expenditure, Employment and Inflation* (Oxford: Blackwell, 1982), p. 116.
5 Interview with Lord Croham.
6 Quoted in W. H. Fishbein, *Wage Restraint by Consensus: Britain's Search for an Incomes Policy Agreement 1965–79* (London: Routledge & Kegan Paul, 1984), p. 104.
7 Cmnd 5125 (1972).
8 Sterling M3 is defined as notes and coins in circulation, together with bank deposits (including certificates of deposit) held by UK residents in both the public and private sectors.
9 Cmnd 5205 (1973), Cmnd 5206 (1973), Cmnd 5247 (1973).
10 Ralph Harris and Brendan Sewill, *British Economic Policy 1970–74. Two Views*, IEA Hobart Paperback No. 7 (London: IEA, 1975), p. 45.
11 *Incomes Data Study*, no. 90, January 1975, p. 16.
12 Samuel Brittan, *How to End the 'Monetarist' Controversy. A Journalist's Reflections on Output, Jobs, Prices and Money* (London: IEA, 1981), pp. 22–4.

Chapter 8: Labour and the Social Contract 1974–9

1 Thomas Balogh, *Labour and Inflation* (London: Fabian Society, 1970).
2 See for example, B. Castle, 'A socialist incomes policy', *New Statesman*, 25 September 1970, p. 4; J. Callaghan, 'The way forward for the trade unions', *AUEW Journal*, January 1971, pp. 2–3; C. A. R. Crosland, 'Time to review Labour policy', *GMWU Journal*, June 1971, p. 3.
3 Labour Party, *Let Us Work Together* (London: Labour Party, 1974), p. 9.
4 J. Barnett, *Inside the Treasury* (London: Deutsch, 1982), pp. 23 and 32.
5 TUC (London: 1974).
6 Labour Party, *Manifesto, October 1974* (London: Labour Party, 1974).
7 Barnett, op. cit., p. 49.
8 Sir Leo Pliatzky, *Getting and Spending. Public Expenditure, Employment and Inflation* (Oxford: Blackwell, 1982), p. 130.
9 J. Haines, *The Politics of Power* (London: Heinemann 1977).
10 ibid.
11 Pliatzky, op. cit., p. 134.
12 Cmnd 6151 (1975).
13 *The Times*, 8 April 1976, p. 15.
14 Cmnd 6507 (1976).
15 Quoted in *Incomes Data Report*, no. 221, November 1975, p. 27.
16 *The Attack on Inflation – After 31st July 1977*, Cmnd 6882 (1977).
17 *Winning the Battle Against Inflation*, Cmnd 7293 (1978).
18 Barnett, op. cit., p. 165.
19 ibid., p. 175.
20 ibid., p. 163.

Chapter 9: The Era of Thatcherism 1979

1 Sir Leo Pliatzky, *Getting and Spending. Public Expenditure, Employment and Inflation* (Oxford: Blackwell, 1982), p. 176.
2 Nigel Lawson, 1984 Mais Lecture, 'The British experiment', quoted in OECD, *United Kingdom Economic Survey* (Paris: OECD, 1985), p. 49.
3 Treasury and Civil Service Committee, *Memoranda on Monetary Policy and Public Expenditure* (HC 450) (London: HMSO, 1980).
4 M1 consists of the notes and coins in circulation, together with sight deposits held in the bank by the private sector. PSL2 consists of notes, coins, bank deposits, other money market instruments and certificates of tax deposit, building society share and deposit accounts, deposits with savings banks and certain National Savings certificates. M0 consists of the notes and coins in circulation.
5 Department of Employment, *Employment. The Challenge for the Nation*, Cmnd 9474 (March 1985), para. 7.18.
6 Quoted in W. Keegan, *Mrs Thatcher's Economic Experiment* (London: Allen Lane, 1984), p. 171.
7 Dept of Employment, op. cit., pars 1.3, 5.2, 7.8.
8 John Hooper, 'The Treasury's sacred cows come in for a roasting', the *Guardian*, 16 October 1985.
9 See Christopher Johnson, 'Rules for fiscal expansion', *Lloyds Bank Economic Bulletin*, no. 80, August 1985.

Chapter 10: Conclusions

1 R. L. Hall, 'Full employment', in C. P. Kindleberger and G. di Tella (eds), *Economics in the Long View*, Vol. 3, *Applications and Cases, Part II* (London: Macmillan, 1982).
2 See Chapter 1, above.
3 See, for example, Lord Kahn, 'Thoughts on the behaviour of wages and monetarism', *Lloyds Bank Review*, n.s., no. 119, January 1976, pp. 2–9.
4 For a more detailed description of tax-based incomes policies see, for example, R. Layard, *More Jobs, Less Inflation* (London: LSE, Institute for Labour Economics, 1982); J. E. Meade, *Stagflation*, Volume 1, *Wage-Fixing* (London: Allen & Unwin, 1982), Chapter 10; N. Bosanquet, 'Tax-based incomes policies', in D. Robinson and K. Mayhew (eds), *Pay Policies for the Future* (Oxford: University Press, 1983).

Select Bibliography

Public Records

Cabinet Office	CAB 21	(Prime Minister's Briefs)
	CAB 24	(Cabinet Papers)
	CAB 58	(Economic Advisory Council Committee on Economic Information)
	CAB 87	(War Cabinet Committees on Post-War Reconstruction)
	CAB 124	(Lord President's Files)
	CAB 128	(Cabinet Conclusions)
	CAB 129	(Cabinet Papers)
	CAB 130	(Cabinet Committees: Minutes and Memoranda)
	CAB 132	(Lord President's Committee and Sub-Committees: Minutes and Memoranda)
	CAB 134	(Cabinet Committees: Minutes and Memoranda)
Foreign Office	FO 800	(Bevin Papers)
Ministry of Labour	LAB 10	(Industrial Relations Files)
Prime Minister's Office	PREM 8	(1945–51)
	PREM 11	(1952–)
Treasury	T 160	(Finance Files)
	T 161	(Supply Files)
	T 171	(Budget Files)
	T 172	(Chancellor's Office: Miscellaneous Papers
	T 175	(Hopkins Papers)
	T 175	(Phillips Papers)
	T 188	(Leith-Ross Papers)
	T 208	(Hawtrey Papers)
	T 227	(Treasury Social Services Division Papers)
	T 229	(Central Economic Planning Staff Papers)
	T 230	(Economic Section Papers)
	T 236	(Treasury Overseas Finance Division Files)
	T 238	(Overseas Negotiations Committee Files)
	T 247	(Keynes Papers)
	T 267	(Treasury Historical Memoranda)
	T 269	(Papers on 1949 Devaluation and Consequent Measures)

Select Bibliography

Private Collections

BRITISH LIBRARY OF POLITICAL AND ECONOMIC SCIENCE
Lord Dalton, Diary and Papers
Professor James Meade, Diary and Papers

CONGRESS HOUSE
TUC Economic Committee Minutes and Memoranda

NUFFIELD COLLEGE, OXFORD
Sir Hubert Henderson Papers

INTERVIEWS
Professor Sir Alec Cairncross
Lord Croham
Professor Stanley Dennison
Professor Sir Donald MacDougall
Lord Plowden
Lord Roberthall
Professor Sir Austin Robinson
Lord Roll
Lord Trend
Miss Nita Watts

Command Papers

Price Stabilisation and Industrial Policy, Cmd 3281 (1941).
The Sources of War Finance, an Analysis and Estimate of the National Income and Expenditure in 1938 and 1940, Cmd 6261 (1941).
Social and Allied Services, Report by Sir William Beveridge, Cmd 6404 (1942).
Employment Policy, Cmd 6527 (1944).
Statement on the Economic Considerations Affecting Relations between Employers and Workers, Cmd 7018 (1947).
Economic Survey (annual, 1947–62).
Statement on Personal Incomes, Costs and Prices, Cmd 7321 (1948).
The Economic Implications of Full Employment, Cmd 9725 (1956).
Council on Prices, Productivity and Incomes (1st–4th Reports, 1958–61).
Report of the Committee on the Working of the Monetary System, Cmnd 827 (1959).
Incomes Policy: The Next Step, Cmnd 1962 (1961).
National Incomes Policy: The Next Step, Cmnd 1626 (1962).
Prices and Incomes Policy, Cmnd 2639 (1965).
Machinery of Prices and Incomes Policy, Cmnd 2577 (1965).
Prices and Incomes: An Early Warning System, Cmnd 2808 (1965).
Prices and Incomes Standstill, Cmnd 3073 (1966).
Prices and Incomes Policy: Period of Severe Restraint, Cmnd 3150 (1966).
Prices and Incomes Policy after 30 June 1967, Cmnd 3235 (1967).

161

NBPI, Report No. 36: Productivity Agreements, Cmnd 3311 (1967).
Productivity, Prices and Incomes Policy in 1968 and 1969, Cmnd 3590 (1968).
Royal Commission on Trade Unions and Employers Associations 1965–8 Report, Cmnd 3623 (1968).
NBPI Report No. 65: Payments by Results Systems, Cmnd 3627 (1968).
In Place of Strife: A Policy for Industrial Relations, Cmnd 3888 (1969).
Productivity, Prices and Incomes Policy After 1969, Cmnd 4237 (1969).
A Programme for Controlling Inflation: The First Stage, Cmnd 5725 (1972).
The Programme for Controlling Inflation: The Second Stage, Cmnd 5205 (1973).
Price and Pay Code. Consultative Document, Cmnd 5247 (1973).
Price and Pay Code for Stage 3. A Consultative Document, Cmnd 5444 (1973).
Pay Board, Advisory Report No. 2. Problems of Pay Relativities, Cmnd 5535 (1974).
Pay Board, Special Report: Relative Pay of Mineworkers, Cmnd 5567 (1974).
The Attack on Inflation, Cmnd 6151 (1975).
The Attack on Inflation – The Second Year, Cmnd 6507 (1976).
The Attack on Inflation – After 31st July 1977, Cmnd 6882 (1977).
Winning the Battle Against Inflation, Cmnd 7293 (1978).
Employment. The Challenge for the Nation, Cmnd 9474 (1985).

Official Publications

OFFICIAL HISTORIES
Hancock, Sir W. K. (ed.), *Statistical Digest of the Second World War* (London: HMSO, 1951).
Hancock, Sir W. K. and Gowing, M. M., *The British War Economy* (London: HMSO, 1949).
Sayers, R. S., *Financial Policy, 1939–45* (London: HMSO, 1956).
Titmuss, R. M., *Problems of Social Policy* (London: HMSO, 1950).

HOUSE OF COMMONS
Parliamentary Debates (Hansard, 5th series).

OTHER OFFICIAL PUBLICATIONS
Central Statistical Office, *Economic Trends* (London: HMSO, various).
Central Statistical Office, *Monthly Digest of Statistics* (London: HMSO, various).
Department of Employment, *British Labour Statistics. Historical Abstract 1886–1968* (London: HMSO, 1971).
Treasury and Civil Service Committee, *Memoranda on Monetary Policy and Public Expenditure*, HC 450 (London: HMSO, 1980); *Monetary Policy*, Vols I–III (London: HMSO, 1981).

Select Bibliography

Newspapers and periodicals

Financial Times
Guardian
Sunday Times
The Economist
The Observer
The Times

Unpublished Sources

Buiter, W. H., 'Monetary policy and international competitiveness', National Bureau of Economic Research Working Paper, no. 591, 1981.
Jones, R. B., 'The wages problem in employment policy 1936–48', M.Sc. thesis, University of Bristol, 1983.
McLeod, R. M., 'The development of full employment policy', PhD thesis, University of Oxford, 1978.
Rollings, N., 'The control of inflation in Britain 1945–53', MS 1985.
Skidelsky, R., 'The Keynesian revolution in historical perspective', MS 1985.
Letters containing replies to various questions were also received from Sir Norman Chester and Professor James Meade.

Published Sources

(Published in London unless otherwise stated)

Addison, J. T. and Burton, J., 'Keynes' analysis of wages and unemployment revisited', *Manchester School*, Vol i, March 1982.
Addison, P., *The Road to 1945* (Quartet, 1977).
Aldcroft, D., *Full Employment: The Elusive Goal* (Harvester Press, 1984).
Ascheim, J., 'From money illusion to money disillusion', *Banco Nationale Del Lavoro Quarterly Review*, Vol xxx, December 1977.
Bain, G. Sayers (ed.), *Industrial Relations in Britain* (Oxford: Blackwell, 1983).
Ball, R. J. and Burns, T., 'The inflationary mechanism in the UK economy', *American Economic Review*, Vol lxvi, 1976.
Balogh, T., *Labour and Inflation* (Fabian Society, 1970).
Balogh, T., *The Irrelevance of Conventional Economics* (Weidenfeld & Nicolson, 1981).
Barnett, J., *Inside the Treasury* (Andre Deutsch, 1982).
Beckerman, W. (ed.), *The Labour Government's Economic Record* (Duckworth, 1972).
Blackaby, F. T. (ed.), *An Incomes Policy for Britain* (Heinemann, 1972).
Blackaby, F. T. (ed.), *British Economic Policy 1960–74, Demand Management* (Cambridge: Cambridge University Press for NIESR, 1978).

163

Booth, A., 'The Keynesian revolution in economic policy making', *Economic History Review*, 2nd series, Vol xxxvi, spring 1982.

Booth, A. and Coats, A. W., 'Some wartime observations on the role of the economist in government', *Oxford Economic Papers*, n.s., Vol xxxii, July 1980.

Bosanquet, N., 'Tax-based incomes policies', in D. Robinson and K. Mayhew (eds.), *Pay Policies for the Future* (Oxford: University Press, 1983).

Bridges, Lord, *The Treasury* (Allen & Unwin, 1966).

Brittan, S., *Steering the Economy* (Harmondsworth: Penguin, 1971).

Brittan, S., 'Full employment policy: a reappraisal', in G. D. N. Worswick (ed.), *The Concept and Measurement of Involuntary Unemployment* (Allen & Unwin, 1976).

Brittan, S., *The Economic Consequences of Democracy* (Temple Smith, 1977).

Brittan, S., *How to End the 'Monetarist' Controversy. A Journalist's Reflections on Output, Jobs, Prices and Money* (IEA, 1981).

Brittan, S. and Lilley, P., *The Delusion of Incomes Policy* (Temple Smith, 1977).

Brown, H. Phelps, *The Origins of Trade Union Power* (Oxford: Oxford University Press, 1983).

Browning, P., *Economic Images. Current Economic Controversies* (Longman, 1983).

Buchanan, J. M., Burton, J. and Wagner, R. E., *The Economic Consequences of Mr Keynes* (IEA, 1983).

Budd, A., 'The development of demand management', in F. Cairncross (ed.), *Changing Perceptions of Economic Policy* (Methuen, 1981).

Buiter, W. H., 'The macroeconomics of Dr Pangloss: a critical survey of the "new Classical" economics', *Economic Journal*, Vol. xc, March 1980.

Bullock, A., *The Life and Times of Ernest Bevin*, Vol. 1, *Trade Union Leader*, and Vol. 2, *Minister of Labour* (Heinemann, 1960 and 1967).

Bullock, A., *Ernest Bevin: Foreign Secretary* (Heinemann, 1984).

Butler, R. A., *The Art of the Possible* (Hamish Hamilton, 1971).

Cairncross, A. K., *Essays in Economic Management* (Allen & Unwin, 1971).

Cairncross, A. K., *Inflation, Growth and International Finance* (Allen & Unwin, 1975).

Cairncross, A. K., 'Keynes and the planned economy', in A. P. Thirlwall (ed.), *Keynes and Laissez-Faire* (Macmillan, 1978).

Cairncross, A. K., 'The relationship between fiscal and monetary policy', *Banco Nationale del Lavoro Quarterly Review*, Vol. xxxiv, December 1981.

Cairncross, A. K., *Years of Recovery. British Economic Policy 1945–53* (Methuen, 1985).

Cairncross, A. K., and Eichengreen, B., *Sterling in Decline: The Devaluations of 1931, 1949 and 1967* (Oxford: Blackwell, 1983).

Cairncross, F. (ed.), *Changing Perceptions of Economic Policy* (Methuen, 1981).

Clark, C., *Taxmanship* (IEA, 1970).

Clarke, R. W. B., *Anglo-American Collaboration in War and Peace 1942–49* (Oxford: Clarendon, 1982).

Clegg, H., *How to Run an Incomes Policy and Why We Made Such a Mess of the Last One* (Oxford: Blackwell, 1971).

164

Clegg, H., *The System of Industrial Relations in Great Britain* (Oxford: Blackwell, 1978).

Coats, A. W., 'Britain: the rise of the socialists', *History of Political Economy*, Vol. xiii, autumn 1981.

Corry, B., 'Keynes in the history of economic thought: some reflections', in A. P. Thirlwall (ed.), *Keynes and Lassez-Faire* (Macmillan, 1978).

Crosland, S., *Tony Crosland* (Cape, 1982).

Donoghue, B. and Jones, B. W., *Herbert Morrison: Portrait of a Politician* (Weidenfeld & Nicolson, 1973).

Dow, J. C. R., *The Management of the British Economy 1945–60* (Cambridge: Cambridge University Press for NIESR, 1964).

Dunlop, J. T., 'The movement of real and money wages', *Economic Journal*, Vol. xlviii, September 1938.

Eatwell, R., *The 1945–51 Labour Governments* (Batsford, 1979).

Eltis, W., 'The failure of the Keynesian conventional wisdom', *Lloyds Bank Review*, n.s., no. 122, October 1976.

Feinstein, C. H., *National Income, Expenditure and Output of the United Kingdom, 1855–1965* (Cambridge: Cambridge University Press, 1972).

Fellner, W. *et al.*, *The Problem of Rising Prices* (Paris: OECC, 1961).

Fender, J., *Understanding Keynes: An Analysis of the General Theory* (Brighton: Wheatsheaf, 1981).

Fishbein, W. H., *Wage Restraint by Concensus. Britain's Search for an Incomes Policy Agreement 1965–79* (Routledge & Kegan Paul, 1984).

Fisher, I., *The Money Illusion* (New York: St Martin's Press, 1928).

Friedman, M., 'The role of monetary policy', *American Economic Review*, Vol. lviii, March 1968.

Friedman, M., *Inflation and Unemployment: The New Dimension of Politics* (IEA, 1977).

Gilbert, J. C., *Keynes Impact on Monetary Economics* (Butterworth, 1982).

Graham, F. D., 'Keynes versus Hayek on a commodity reserve currency', *Economic Journal*, Vol. liv, December 1944.

Haines, J., *The Politics of Power* (London: Heinemann, 1977).

Hall, R. L., 'Britain's economic problems', *The Economist*, 16 September 1961 and 23 September 1961.

Hall, R. L., 'Incomes policy – state of play', *Three Banks Review*, March 1964.

Hall, R. L., 'Full employment', in C. P. Kindleberger and G. di Tella (eds), *Economics in the Long View*, Vol. 3, *Applications and Cases, Part II* (Macmillan, 1982).

Harris, R. and Sewill, B., *British Economic Policy 1970–74. Two Views* (IEA, 1975).

Harrod, R. F., 'Retrospect on Keynes', in R. Lekachman (ed.), *Keynes' General Theory: Reports of Three Decades* (New York: St Martin's Press, 1964).

Harrod, R. F., 'Keynes' theory and its application', in D. E. Moggridge (ed.), *Keynes: Aspects of the Man and his Work* (Macmillan, 1974).

Hawkins, K., *British Industrial Relations 1945–75* (Barrie & Jenkins, 1976).

Hayek, F. A. von, *Monetary Nationalism and International Stability* (Geneva: 1937).

Hayek, F. A. von, 'A commodity reserve currency', *Economic Journal*, Vol. liii, March 1943.

Hayek, F. A. von, *A Tiger by the Tail* (IEA, 1977).

Henderson, H. D. (ed. Sir H. Clay), *The Inter-War Years and Other Papers* (Oxford University Press, 1955).

Hicks, J. R., *Value and Capital* (Oxford: Clarendon, 1939).

Hicks, J. R., *The Crisis in Keynesian Economics* (Oxford: Blackwell, 1974).

Hicks, J. R., 'What is wrong with monetarism', *Lloyds Bank Review*, n.s., no. 118, October 1975.

Hicks, J. R., *Economic Perspectives* (Oxford: Clarendon, 1977).

Hopkin, B., 'The development of demand management', in F. Cairncross (ed.), *Changing Perceptions of Economic Policy* (Methuen, 1981).

Howard, A. (ed.), *The Crossman Diaries* (condensed version) (Methuen, 1981).

Howson, S., *Domestic Monetary Management, 1919–1938* (Cambridge: Cambridge University Press, 1975).

Howson, S., 'Slump and unemployment', in R. Floud and D. McCloskey (eds), *The Economic History of Britain since 1700, Part II* (Cambridge: Cambridge University Press, 1981).

Howson, S. and Winch, D., *The Economic Advisory Council 1930–39: A Study in Economic Advice during Depressing and Recovery* (Cambridge: Cambridge University Press, 1977).

Hutchison, T. W., *Keynes versus the 'Keynesians' . . . ?* (IEA, 1977).

Hutchison, T. W., *On Revolutions and Progress in Economic Knowledge* (Cambridge: Cambridge University Press, 1978).

Hutchison, T. W., *The Politics and Philosophy of Economics* (Oxford: Blackwell, 1981).

Hutt, W. H., *The Keynesian Episode: A Reassessment* (Indianapolis, Ind.: Liberty Press, 1979).

IMF, *International Financial Statistics* (New York: IMF, yearly).

Jarrat, A. A., 'A workable incomes policy for Britain', in F. T. Blackaby (ed.), *An Incomes Policy for Britain* (Heinemann, 1972).

Jay, D., *Change and Fortune. A Political Record* (Hutchinson, 1980).

Jay, P., 'Inflation, full employment and the threat to democracy', in IEA, *Inflation: Causes, Consequences and Cures. Discourses on the Debate between the Monetary and Trade Union Interpretations* (IEA, 1974).

Jewkes, J., 'A defence of the White Paper on employment policy 1944', in *A Return to Free Market Economics? Critical Essays on Government Intervention* (Macmillan, 1978).

Jones, A., *The New Inflation: the Politics of Prices and Incomes* (Harmondsworth: Penguin, 1973).

Kahn, Lord, 'Lord Keynes and contemporary economic problems', in *Essays on Employment and Growth* (Cambridge University Press, 1972).

Kahn, Lord, 'On re-reading Keynes', *Proceedings of the British Academy*, Vol. lx, 1974.

Kahn, Lord, 'Unemployment as seen by Keynesians', in G. D. N. Worswick (ed.), *The Concept and Measurement of Involuntary Unemployment* (Allen & Unwin, 1976).

Kahn, Lord, 'Thoughts on the behaviour of wages and monetarism', *Lloyds Bank Review*, n.s., no. 119, January 1976.

Kahn, Lord, 'On the development of Keynes' thought', *Journal of Economic Literature*, Vol. xvi, June 1978.

Kaldor, Lord, *The Scourge of Monetarism* (Oxford: Oxford University Press, 1982).

Kaldor, Lord, *The Economic Consequences of Mrs Thatcher* (Duckworth, 1983).

Kalecki, M., 'The budget and inflation', *Bulletin of the Oxford Institute of Statistics*, Vol. xiii, April 1941.

Keegan, W., *Mrs Thatcher's Economic Experiment* (Allen Lane, 1984).

Keegan, W. and Penant-Rea, R., *Who Runs the Economy? Control and Influence in British Economic Policy* (Temple Smith, 1979).

Keynes, J. M., *The Collected Writings of John Maynard Keynes* (hereafter *Collected Writings*), Vol. ii, *The Economic Consequences of the Peace* (Macmillan, 1971).

Keynes, J. M., *Collected Writings*, Vol. vii, *The General Theory of Employment, Interest and Money* (Macmillan, 1973).

Keynes, J. M., *Collected Writings*, Vol. xiii, *The General Theory and After: Part I. Preparation* (Macmillan, 1973).

Keynes, J. M., *Collected Writings*, Vol. xiv, *The General Theory and After: Part II. Defence and Development* (Macmillan, 1973).

Keynes, J. M., *Collected Writings*, Vol. xxii, *Activities 1939–45: Internal War Finance* (Macmillan, 1980).

Keynes, J. M., *Collected Writings*, Vol. xxvi, *Activities 1941–46: Shaping the Post-War World: Bretton Woods and Reparations* (Macmillan, 1980).

Keynes, J. M., *Collected Writings*, Vol. xxvii, *Activities 1940–46: Shaping the Post-War World: Employment and Commodities* (Macmillan, 1980).

Keynes, J. M., *Collected Writings*, Vol. xxix, *The General Theory and After: A Supplement* (Macmillan, 1979).

Keynes, J. M., 'The relative movements of real wages and output', *Economic Journal*, vol. liv, March 1939.

Keynes, J. M., 'How to avoid a slump', *The Times*, 12, 13 and 14 Jauary 1937.

Keynes, J. M., 'Borrowing for defence: is it inflation?', *The Times*, 11 March 1937.

Keynes, M. (ed.), *Essays on John Maynard Keynes* (Cambridge: Cambridge University Press, 1975).

Labour Party, *Full Employment and Financial Policy* (Labour Party, 1945).

Labour Party, *Let Us Face the Future* (Labour Party, 1945).

Labour Party, *Let Us Work Together* (Labour Party, 1974).

Labour Party, *Manifesto, October 1974* (Labour Party, 1974).

Layard, R., 'Is incomes policy the answer to unemployment?', *Economica*, n.s., Vol. xlix, August 1982.

Lekachman, R. (ed.), *Keynes' General Theory: Reports of Three Decades* (New York: St Martin's Press, 1964).

Leontieff, W., 'The fundamental assumption of Mr Keynes' monetary theory of employment', *Quarterly Journal of Economics*, Vol. xlix, November 1936.

167

Lerner, A. P., 'Employment theory and employment policy', *American Economic Review*, Vol. lvii, March 1967.

Marwick, A., 'Middle opinion in the nineteen-thirties: planning, progress and political agreement', *English Historical Review*, Vol. lxxix, April 1964.

Mathews, R. C. O. and Sargent, J. R. (eds), *Contemporary Problems of Economic Policy. Essays from the Clare Group* (Methuen, 1983).

Meade, J. E., *An Introduction to Economic Analysis and Policy* (Oxford: Clarendon, 1936).

Meade, J. E., *Stagflation*, Vol. 1, *Wage Fixing* (Allen & Unwin, 1982).

Meltzer, A., 'On Keynes' general theory', *Journal of Economic Literature*, Vol. xix, March 1981.

Middleton, R., 'The Treasury in the nineteen-thirties: political and administrative constraints to the acceptance of the "new" economics', *Oxford Economic Papers*, n.s., Vol. xxxiv, March 1982.

Moggridge, D. E., 'New light on post-war plans', *The Banker*, Vol. cxxii, March 1972.

Moggridge, D. E., (ed.), *Keynes, Aspects of the Man and his Work* (Macmillan, 1972).

Moggridge, D. E., 'Economic policy in the Second World War', in M. Keynes (ed.), *Essays on John Maynard Keynes* (Cambridge: Cambridge University Press, 1975).

Moggridge, D. E., *Keynes* (Fontana, 1976).

Moggridge, D. E. and Howson, S., 'Keynes on monetary policy', *Oxford Economic Papers*, Vol. xxvi, July 1974.

National Institute of Economic and Social Research Review (quarterly, various issues).

OECD, *United Kingdom Economic Survey* (Paris: OECD, 1985).

Parker, R. A. C., 'British rearmament, 1936–9: Treasury, trade unions and skilled labour', *English Historical Review*, Vol. xcvi, April 1981.

Patinkin, D., 'Keynes' monetary thought: a study of its development', *History of Political Economy*, Vol. iii, winter 1976.

Peden, G. C., *British Rearmament and the Treasury 1932–39* (Edinburgh: Scottish Academic Press, 1979).

Peden, G. C., 'Keynes, the Treasury and unemployment in the later nineteen-thirties', *Oxford Economic Papers*, n.s., vol. xxxii, March 1980.

Peden, G. C., 'Sir Richard Hopkins and the "Keynesian revolution" in employment policy', *Economic History Review*, 2nd series, Vol. xxxvi, 1983.

Peden, G. C., *British Economic and Social Policy, Lloyd George to Margaret Thatcher* (Oxford: Philip Allan, 1985).

Phelps, E. S., 'Phillips Curves, expectations of inflation and optimal unemployment over time', *Economica*, n.s., Vol. xxxiv, August 1967.

Phillips, A. W., 'The relationship between unemployment and the rate of change of money wages in the United Kingdom, 1861–1957', *Economica*, n.s., Vol. xxv, November 1958.

Pliatzky, Sir Leo, *Getting and Spending. Public Expenditure, Employment and Inflation* (Oxford: Blackwell, 1982).

Pollard, S., *The Development of the British Economy 1914–67* (Edward Arnold, 1976).

Robbins, Lord, *Autobiography of an Economist* (Macmillan, 1971).
Roberts, B. C., *National Wages Policy in War and Peace* (Allen & Unwin, 1958).
Robinson, E. A. G., 'Keynes; economist, author, statesman', *Proceedings of the British Academy*, Vol. lvii, 1971.
Roll, Lord, *Crowded Hours* (Faber, 1985).
Sayers, R. S., *The Bank of England III, 1891–1944* (Cambridge: Cambridge University Press, 1976).
Seldon, A., *Churchill's Indian Summer. The Conservative Government 1951–55* (Hodder & Stoughton, 1981).
Shonfield, A. (ed. Z. Shonfield), *The Use of Public Power* (Oxford: Oxford University Press, 1982).
Skidelsky, R. (ed.), *The End of the Keynesian Era. Essays on the Disintegration of the Keynesian Political Economy* (Macmillan, 1978).
Solow, R. M., 'On theories of unemployment', *American Economic Review*, Vol. lxx, March 1980.
Thirlwall, A. P. (ed.), *Keynes and Laissez-Faire* (Macmillan, 1978).
Trevithick, J. A., 'Keynes, inflation and money illusion', *Economic Journal*, Vol. lxxxv, March 1975.
Trevithick, J. A., *Inflation* (Penguin, 1977).
TUC, *Interim Report on Post-War Reconstruction* (TUC, 1944).
TUC, *A Policy for Real Wages* (TUC, 1948).
TUC, *Productivity, Prices and Incomes: Report of a Conference of Executive Committees of Affiliated Organisations Held on 30 April 1965* (TUC, 1965).
TUC, *The Chequers and Downing Street Talks* (TUC, 1972).
TUC, *Collective Bargaining and the Social Contract* (TUC, 1974).
TUC, *Annual Report* (TUC, various issues).
TUC, *Economic Review* (TUC, various issues).
Vines, D., Maciejowski, J., Meade, J. E., *Stagflation*, Vol. 2, *Demand Management* (Allen & Unwin, 1983).
Williams, P. M. (ed.), *The Diary of Hugh Gaitskell 1945–1956* (Cape, 1983).
Wilson, H., *The Labour Government 1964–70. A Personal Record* (Weidenfeld & Nicolson, 1971).
Wilson, T., *Policy in War and Peace: The Recommendations of J. M. Keynes* (Glasgow: University of Glasgow Press, 1981).
Winch, D., *Economics and Policy* (Glasgow: Collins, 1972).
Wood, J. B., *How Little Unemployment?* (IEA, 1975).
Worswick, G. D. N. (ed.), *The British Economy 1945–60* (Oxford: Clarendon, 1956).
Worswick, G. D. N., *The Concept and Measurement of Involuntary Unemployment* (Allen & Unwin, 1956).
Worswick, G. D. N. and Ady, P. H. (eds), *The British Economy in the Nineteen-Fifties* (Oxford: Oxford University Press, 1962).

Index

170

Index

United States 92, 97
United States Treasury
    UK Incomes Policy, and 20–1

VAT 93, 101
    introduction of 83
    raising of (1979) 121, 125

wage drift 46, 77–9, 93, 139–40
wage explosion of 1969–70 79–81
Wages Advisory Council 38–41, 42
Wages Councils 43, 125

Williams, Shirley 105, 106
Williamson, Tom 45
Wilson, Harold (Lord Wilson) 42, 66, 71,
    96–7, 114–15, 124
    Devaluation of 1967 and 75
    In Place of Strife and 78
    Social Contract and 100–1, 105
Winter of Discontent 112–14
Wood, Sir Kingsley 23
Woodcock, George 46, 68, 70
    'Guiding Light' and 59
    Early Warning System and 71

175

For Product Safety Concerns and Information please contact our EU
representative GPSR@taylorandfrancis.com
Taylor & Francis Verlag GmbH, Kaufingerstraße 24, 80331 München, Germany

9 780367 024925